Quick After-Work

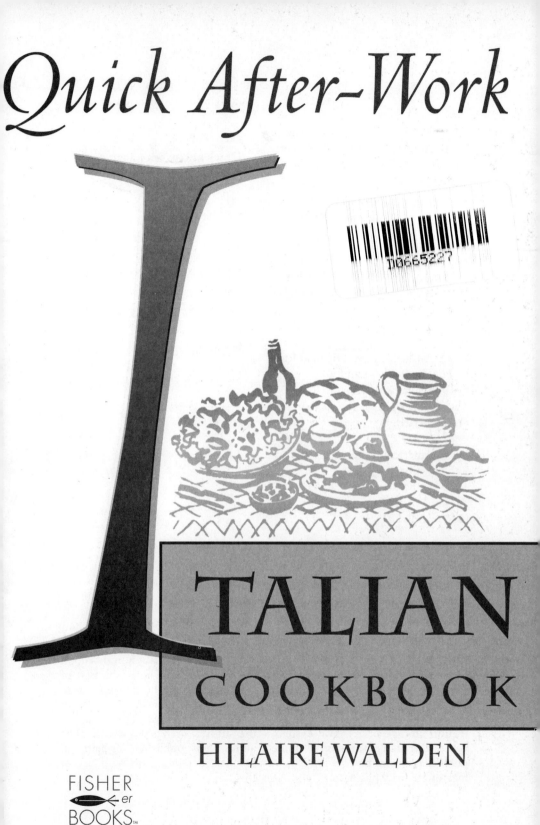

ITALIAN
COOKBOOK

HILAIRE WALDEN

FISHER
BOOKS™

Publishers:	Bill Fisher
	Howard Fisher
	Helen V. Fisher
North American Editors:	Helen V. Fisher
	Sarah Smith
Cover Design:	FifthStreet*design*
Back Cover Photo:	James Murphy
Book Design:	Josh Young
Illustrations:	Madeleine David
Book Production:	Deanie Wood
Nutrient Analysis:	Miriam Fisher

Library of Congress
Cataloging-in-Publication Data

Walden, Hilaire.
    Quick after-work Italian cook-
book / Hilaire Walden.
      p. cm.
    Includes index.
    ISBN 1-55561-109-5 (pb)
    1. Cookery, Italian. 2. Quick and
easy cookery. I. Title.
TX723.W24 1996
641.5'55--dc20   96-23901
                                CIP

First published in Great Britain in 1995
by Piatkus Books, London
© 1995 Hilaire Walden
The moral right of the author has
been asserted.

North American Edition
Published by Fisher Books
4239 W. Ina Road, Suite #101
Tucson, AZ 85741
(520) 744-6110

© 1996 Hilaire Walden
Printed in USA
Printing 10 9 8 7 6 5 4 3 2 1

Notice: The information in this book is true and complete to the best of our knowledge. The information in this book is general and is offered with no guarantees on the part of the author or Fisher Books. The author and publisher disclaim all liability in connection with use of this book.

Contents

INTRODUCTION

Italians have an inherent love of good food, and even meals that are prepared quickly are prepared with care and attention. Italians shop with knowledge and discrimination, selecting only top-quality, natural produce that bursts with abundant flavor. Tasty ingredients are combined with flair and cooked with skill to make dishes that, according to style, ooze or explode with exuberant flavor—zesty lemon, fragrant basil, piquant capers or salty anchovies.

Even with changing lifestyles and food preferences, Italian cooks tend to steer away from creativity for creativity's sake, preferring to stay with tradition and the local dishes of their region, town or village. This does not mean that they are opposed to change, but that innovations are composed with care and sensitivity, making the most sympathetic use of the best ingredients. You will find the recipes in this book conform to the characteristic style that has made Italian food so popular.

The recipes can be prepared quickly, with a minimum of effort, and they cook quickly as well. All the dishes will be ready to eat in under 30 minutes and many in less time than that.

To make meal preparation and cooking as straightforward and as quick as possible, plan ahead and keep a few guidelines in mind. Choose recipes whose preparation and cooking fit easily together. For example, team a first course that has to be prepared and cooked at the last minute with an entrée that can be prepared ahead of time and left to cook. Conversely, choose a simple first course that requires little or no cooking to precede an entrée that calls for more attention. Accompany such a main course with a plain or simply cooked vegetable. If you are using the oven for one dish, choose another that can also be baked.

Before starting to prepare a meal, check that you have all the ingredients you will need. Remove them from the refrigerator, if necessary, so they can start to reach room temperature; cold ingredients take longer to cook. Then read through the entire recipe to find out when to preheat the broiler or bring water to a boil, which ingredients to prepare first and which can be prepared while others are cooking. This won't take long and you may remember all of it so that you won't have to break off in the middle of cooking to find out what to do next.

Cooking times vary according to the ingredients being used. Young vegetables cook more speedily than old ones, and small or thin pieces of food cook more quickly than large or fat ones. Diced butter melts more rapidly and evenly than a single piece. The temperature of the equipment when you start to cook, as well as that of the ingredients, will also affect the cooking time.

Please regard my recipes as guides and adapt them if you like. The measurements suited my taste and that of my friends when I tested the recipes. But the flavors of fresh ingredients are not constant, brand-name products vary, and everyone has his or her personal preferences. Get into the habit of tasting while preparing a dish and before serving it—this is the simplest of skills to learn from good cooks.

INGREDIENTS

Sun-dried tomatoes, once a rarity, are easily available today, as are pesto and savory pastes such as black-olive. I live in a small, rural town, yet bought everything I needed for this book in the vicinity. If you can't find what you want in a local supermarket, try delicatessens or a mail-order company that specializes in unusual ingredients.

Keep the following items in your cupboard as ammunition for inspiration in creating quick, tasty dishes.

BALSAMIC VINEGAR

Although it has recently become fashionable, balsamic vinegar has been made for hundreds of years. Its rich, sweet, nutty taste is due to the special way it is made. Mashed grapes are cooked, then fermented over a period of years in a succession of barrels made from different woods.

The vinegar should be at least four or five years old when it is sold, and may be up to 40 years or more. Because they evaporate and concentrate as they mature, older vinegars become thicker and the flavor richer. They also become progressively more expensive; even young balsamic vinegars are not cheap.

Balsamic vinegar is more like a condiment or seasoning than a standard vinegar; just a few drops add a unique, sweet-sour flavor to salad dressings and sauces. Always add it toward the end of cooking because overheating spoils the flavor. Try sprinkling a few drops over grilled meats and poultry to give them a quick lift.

BREADS

The range and quality of breads available in supermarkets and bakeries has improved enormously in recent years, and it is now possible to buy very good, firm-textured, well-flavored Italian breads such as *ciabatta* and *foccacia*. If you cannot find these breads, use any other similar bread, such as French country bread (*pain de campagne*).

CHEESES

DOLCELATTE—A smooth, blue-veined, mild, factory-produced cheese made by the firm of Galbani. The name is a registered trademark.

FONTINA—This semisoft cheese is smooth, with a delicate, sweet, nutlike flavor. Inside its golden-brown rind the pale yellow interior is often dotted with small holes. A delicious accompaniment to fresh fruit, fontina also melts easily and smoothly for use in cooked dishes.

GOAT CHEESE—Cheeses made from goat's milk come in a variety of shapes, and range in texture from moist and creamy to dry and semi-firm. Pure white in color, they have a tart flavor and are often coated with herbs or black pepper.

GORGONZOLA—This has the texture of ripe brie. Its blue-green marbling contrasts beautifully with the creaminess of the cheese. Depending on the variety, gorgonzola can be quite mild or fairly piquant. It should never be strong or taste of ammonia.

MASCARPONE—A voluptuous, velvety, fresh cheese with a mild, slightly sweet taste, mascarpone is sold in tubs in the dairy section of supermarkets. It should be used soon after purchase or the flavor will deteriorate. It is expensive.

MOZZARELLA—Genuine mozzarella is made from the milk of water buffaloes and has a more pronounced, yet delicate, fresher flavor than the cow's milk version. It is also more compact and whiter, and will "ooze" tears of whey when cut.

PARMESAN—True Parmigiano Reggiano can only be made between May and November, from cow's milk from designated provinces. Its manufacture is governed by strict laws, and the name appears on the cheese.

Never buy cardboard containers of grated Parmesan—the taste and texture are far removed from those of the true product. Buy it by the piece and grate it as needed.

PECORINO—This hard cheese is made from sheep's milk. It is produced all over the south of Italy and can vary in flavor and piquancy. Pecorino is a good cheese for grating or cutting into slivers.

RICOTTA—Made from the whey from other cheeses, ricotta should be eaten very fresh, when it has a delicate, clean, fresh taste; it quite quickly begins to taste rancid.

GARLIC

It is impossible to do much Italian cooking without using garlic. Remember that the quick cooking times in this book mean the flavor will be at its most pronounced (it mellows with long, slow cooking). For a milder taste, use whole or halved cloves rather than chopped or crushed ones. When cooking dishes in oil, you can fry the garlic first to add flavor, then remove it before putting in other ingredients.

I buy loose bulbs rather than those that are prepacked because I find they keep better. It is also easier to check that the individual cloves are plump and firm. Keep garlic in a cool, dry, airy place. If any green shoots start to appear, cut the clove lengthwise before using it and discard the shoots, which taste bitter.

HERBS

With the exception of oregano, fresh herbs have a far superior taste to dried ones and, as they are now so readily available, there is no reason for not using them. It is also very easy to grow basic herbs such as parsley and chives, even if you do not have a garden—a window box or pots on a sunny window sill will suffice.

If you really cannot get fresh herbs, choose freeze-dried or frozen ones, both of which are sold in supermarkets.

The flavor and pungency of any fresh herb will vary with its growing conditions and time of year. Therefore, quantities given in recipes can only be guides. It is worth getting into the habit of tasting herbs before using them to judge their flavor and strength and adjust amounts. Don't forget to taste the dish at the end of cooking so you can fine-tune the flavor if necessary.

Keep freshly cut herbs in vegetable-storage bags. If you have more than you need, freeze them in small quantities.

I use the flat-leaf, or Italian, parsley.

OLIVE OIL

A burgeoning range of olive oils of different styles and varying qualities is now available. Choice is a matter of personal preference and the use to which the oil is to be put. Store olive oils in a cool, dark place but preferably not in the refrigerator.

The color of an oil is no indication of quality—a rich dark green does not necessarily mean it is superior—but it is an indication of the amount of flavor it contains.

The taste, texture and color of the oils vary according to the type of olives used, where they have grown and ripened, their degree of ripeness when picked and how they have been handled and pressed. Tuscan oils, for example, are peppery, grassy and green while Ligurian ones are golden, delicate and light. To add variety to your cooking, buy small bottles of different types.

In descending order of quality, purity, intensity of flavor and price, the grades in which olive oils are sold are:

EXTRA-VIRGIN OIL—This results from the first pressing of the olives, and has the lowest acidity and, therefore, the most rounded flavor. Commercially produced extra-virgin oils are blended from different oils and always taste the same. Those produced by estates, farms and village cooperatives have their own individual characters and, because they are unblended, will vary from year to year like the best estate-bottled wines.

I use light extra-virgin oil for salad dressings or when only small quantities of oil are required. Richer, more full-bodied oil is used for brushing on meats and poultry before grilling, tossing with pasta, trickling over firm-textured bread or toast or stirring into soups.

VIRGIN OIL—This comes from the second pressing of the olives. It is good for dressing salads and for most cooking.

OLIVE OIL—This used to be called *pure olive oil* and is a blend of virgin olive oil and refined oils obtained by chemical extraction. I use it primarily for cooking.

OLIVE PASTES

These are made with puréed olives—black or green—and olive oil. They are usually flavored with herbs and sometimes with garlic and anchovies.

I keep a jar of black-olive paste in my cupboard. It comes in very handy for spreading on crostini or pizza crusts, combining with crème fraîche to make an instant sauce for pasta, and livening up salad dressings.

PANCETTA

Like bacon, pancetta is made from pork belly. Also like bacon, it has layers of fat and lean meat. Most pancetta is cured, but some is smoked. *Pancetta stesa* is left in its natural shape like bacon. *Pancetta arrotala* is leaner and is flavored with cloves and pepper and rolled.

Pancetta can be substituted for prosciutto in cooking. Pancetta arrotala is the best one to slice and serve at the table, but in this case it is not a substitute for prosciutto.

PASTA

Many fresh pastas are available, but fresh does not necessarily mean better—some dried pastas are better than some fresh ones. However, good fresh pasta is deliciously light and almost melts in the mouth.

PESTO

Commercially produced bottled and fresh pesto sauces are available. They vary in taste, texture and quality; some are close to the home-made version, others are inferior. It is not difficult to make your own pesto, and it is worth making in summer when the flavor of basil is at its best. Using the traditional mortar and pestle produces pesto with the best flavor and texture but is a little laborious. The speed and ease of using a blender or food processor outweigh the loss in quality for many people, but for me the loss is too great.

If you make a lot of pesto, pack it into small, airtight containers and refrigerate it, allowing it to come to room temperature before using. You may also freeze it in ice-cube trays and keep the cubes in a plastic bag, ready to be thawed in the refrigerator as needed. When I make pesto for freezing I prefer not to add the cheese until the sauce has thawed.

The classic way of using pesto is with *trenette,* the local Ligurian fettucine, but there are innumerable other uses—spooned onto sliced tomatoes; served with plainly cooked meats, poultry and fish; added to sauces, casseroles and soups; as a filling for rolled fish fillets; or mixed with soft cheese and slipped between the skin and flesh of a chicken or chicken portions.

PROSCIUTTO AND PARMA HAM

Prosciutto crudo, usually just labeled "prosciutto," is cured and salted raw ham. It is produced throughout Italy in various styles and qualities. According to strict regulations, Parma ham can only be made around Parma. It is generally considered the best prosciutto, although some aficionados prefer San Daniele.

STOCK

I urge you to use real stock, not stock made from a cube. It is very easy to make: In a large kettle, cover chicken skin and bones with water, add an onion, a carrot, a stick of celery and a fresh bouquet garni (sprigs of thyme and parsley and a bay leaf tied together or placed in a cheesecloth bag and discarded after cooking). Simmer 20 to 40 minutes. If you do not need stock within the next day or so, strain and freeze it. You can freeze skin and bones and make stock with them when you have time.

Fish stock is made the same way, but is simmered only 20 minutes.

Make vegetable stock by softening and lightly browning an onion in olive oil, then adding sliced leek, carrot and celery, some mushroom stalks and tomato skins and seeds and a bunch of fresh herbs. Cover with water and simmer 20 to 40 minutes.

Freeze homemade stock in 1-cup (250ml) amounts for added convenience. Be sure to label and date containers. Use within 6 months.

SUN-DRIED TOMATOES

Look for a reputable brand of plump, well-flavored tomatoes dried naturally under the hot sun. Price can be a good guide—cheap sun-dried tomatoes will not be genuine. Those preserved in olive oil are more expensive than dry ones.

To have a supply of the dried variety ready for use, soak several at a time until they are plumped up, then drain them, dry them with paper towels and layer them in a jar with olive oil. Seal the jar and keep in a cool, dark place.

The oil from sun-dried tomatoes can be used in salad dressings or brushed on bread, toast or pizza.

SUN-DRIED-TOMATO PASTE

Because it is made from sun-dried tomatoes, this paste has a richer, more intense taste than tomato purée and I find it much better for boosting the flavor of tomato sauces. It adds depth and character to the flavor of sauces and salad dressings. It can also be spread on breads and pizzas, or it can be tossed with pasta.

TOMATOES

Store-bought tomatoes used to be universally flavorless but this dire situation is beginning to be redressed with supermarkets competing for the most flavorful tomatoes. It is also becoming easier to buy good locally grown tomatoes in season.

To skin and seed tomatoes, plunge into boiling water to cover, leave 1 minute and drain. When cool enough to handle, slip off the skins. Cut in half and scoop or squeeze out the seeds.

EQUIPMENT

The amount and complexity of the equipment you will need for my recipes is minimal. The occasions when I have little time for cooking are also those when I don't want to spend much time cleaning up. Although specialty items are not needed, here are a few utensils you may find helpful.

BLENDERS—I have a small blender as well as a normal-size one, which I find too large for many tasks, especially if I am cooking for just two people. I use my bigger blender instead of a food processor for puréeing soups and sauces—the results are better and a blender is considerably easier to wash.

KNIVES—Contrary to the often-stated opinion, it is not vital to have a set of expensive, really sharp knives. True, these do speed up chopping and slicing, but to gain most benefit from them you have to be able to use them proficiently. It is also true that a dull knife is inefficient. You can probably manage with one or two reasonably sharp knives. I know I do!

MANDOLINE SLICER/GRATER—This can be made of metal, wood or plastic, with adjustable steel blades for slicing and grating vegetables. I use my mandoline more than my food processor for these tasks because it does not reduce foods like onions to a watery mass, takes up less room and is easier to wash. A mandoline also costs less than a food processor.

MEZZALUNA—A mezzaluna, also called a *crescent cutter,* is a two-handled, sickle-shaped blade that is useful for speedily chopping ingredients such as herbs, garlic and onions. Mezzalunas are available in a range of sizes.

POTATO PEELER—This is very handy for shaving Parmesan cheese.

LARGE SAUCEPAN—You will need this in order to cook pasta properly. As a general guide, you should have a saucepan large enough to hold 1 quart (1 liter) of boiling water for every 4 ounces (115g) of pasta.

HEATPROOF COLANDER—This is necessary for draining pasta quickly. It can also be used for steaming.

SKILLETS—I advise having one large and one small heavy-based skillet. Nonstick surfaces assist both cooking and washing, but they can be damaged if you are cooking over very high heat, especially if the pan is dry.

NOTES ABOUT THE RECIPES

I have given both U.S. and metric measurements, but it is important to follow either one or the other. Don't mix U. S. and metric.

Unless otherwise stated I use moderate heat for broiling, grilling and frying.

Herbs are fresh unless stated otherwise.

NUTRIENT ANALYSIS

Nutrient analysis was calculated using The Food Processor® for Windows software program, version 6.0, copyright 1987-1995 by ESHA Research.

Analysis does not include optional ingredients or variations. Where an ingredient amount is a range, the higher number is used. Where the number of servings is a range, the lower number is used. 2% milk was assumed in all recipes using milk.

The following abbreviations are used:

Cal = Calories

Prot = Protein

Carb = Carbohydrates

Fib = Fiber

Tot. Fat = Total Fat

Sat. Fat = Saturated Fat

Chol = Cholesterol

MENUS

Arugula, Tomato and Mozzarella Salad

Chicken with Savory Basil Sauce
Sautéed Red Peppers

Cappuccino Creams

———◦∞◦———

Spinach Soup

Lamb Cutlets with Rosemary
Glazed Leeks Parmesan

Italian Raspberry Layer

———◦∞◦———

Eggs with Tuna Sauce

Pasta with Broccoli and Gorgonzola

Meringue-Topped Stuffed Peaches

———◦∞◦———

***

Bagna Cauda

Fish with Polenta Crust
Simple green salad

Ice Cream with Espresso

***

Broiled Artichoke Salad

Steak with Tomatoes and Olives

Mascarpone with Fruit

***

Stuffed Mushrooms

Fish with Zucchini
Herb-Topped Tomatoes (cooked in the oven)

Summer Berries

Chapter One

FIRST COURSES AND SNACKS

Traditionally an evening meal in Italy is preceded by small, tasty dishes known as *antipasti*. These also make ideal first courses and snacks. Two or more can be combined to serve as a main course.

I find Italian soups very useful because they are speedy and uncomplicated to prepare. The recipes are conveniently adaptable, and a soup can easily be transformed into a light meal by adding croutons or serving with bread and a salad.

You will find other recipes suitable for first courses and snacks in chapter 2.

CAULIFLOWER-PARMESAN SOUP

Serve croutons with this soup to add an appetizing, contrasting crunch.

2-1/3 cups (580ml) vegetable or
   chicken stock
1 medium cauliflower
1/2 cup (125ml) milk or cream

Freshly grated nutmeg to taste
2-3 tablespoons freshly grated
   Parmesan cheese
Salt and pepper to taste

1. Bring stock to a boil. Divide cauliflower into florets, discarding tough parts of stalk. Chop remaining stalks. Add all cauliflower pieces to stock, cover and simmer until very tender.
2. Pour soup into food processor or blender, add milk or cream and process until it is the desired texture.
3. Return soup to pan and stir in nutmeg, Parmesan, salt and pepper. Reheat gently; do not allow to boil.

Makes 4 servings.

Each serving contains:

Cal	Prot	Carb	Fib	Tot. Fat	Sat. Fat	Chol	Sodium
66	5g	8g	2g	3g	2g	6mg	191mg

Croutons ~ *Cut day-old bread into cubes and cook until golden and crisp, either by sautéing in olive oil or by tossing with olive oil and baking in a 325F (160C) oven.*

SPINACH SOUP

To make the soup more creamy, reduce the quantity of milk slightly and either add a couple of tablespoons of mascarpone cheese when puréeing the spinach, or add a spoonful of warmed mascarpone to each bowl as the soup is served. Add an interesting texture contrast by tossing warm croutons, page 2, with Parmesan cheese and serving them with the soup.

4 tablespoons (60g) unsalted
  butter
1 large leek, sliced
1-1/4 lb. (575g) fresh spinach
2-1/3 cups (580ml) vegetable or
  chicken stock

2-1/3 cups (580ml) milk
1 oz. (30g) freshly grated
  Parmesan cheese (1/4 cup)
Freshly grated nutmeg to taste
Salt and pepper to taste

1. Heat butter in a saucepan, add leek and cook until softened. Stir in spinach, cover and cook until wilted. Pour in stock, bring to a boil, cover and simmer 10 minutes.
2. Transfer spinach and some of the stock to a blender and purée. Return to pan, stir in milk and add Parmesan, nutmeg, salt and pepper. Reheat gently but do not boil.

Makes 4 servings.

Each serving contains:

Cal	Prot	Carb	Fib	Tot. Fat	Sat. Fat	Chol	Sodium
281	13g	20g	6g	17g	11g	47mg	396mg

TOMATO-BREAD SOUP

I find that 2 cups (115g) of bread is about right, particularly in summer, but some people add more to make a more-substantial soup. If you prefer, omit the breadcrumbs and put a slice of toasted bread in each soup bowl before pouring in the soup; let stand for a minute, then serve with freshly grated Parmesan cheese.

3 tablespoons olive oil
1 onion, chopped
1 clove garlic, chopped
1-1/2 lb. (700g) tomatoes,
  quartered
2-1/2 cups (625ml) vegetable
  stock

1-1/2 tablespoons sun-dried-
  tomato paste or tomato purée,
  or to taste
2 cups (115g) soft torn
  breadcrumbs
1 cup chopped basil
Salt and pepper to taste

1. Heat oil in saucepan, add onion and cook gently until golden and softened. Add garlic toward the end of cooking.
2. Stir in tomatoes, stock and tomato paste or purée and bring to a boil. Partially cover the pan and simmer about 20 minutes.
3. Add breadcrumbs and most of the basil just before the end of cooking.
4. Add salt and pepper to taste and garnish with remaining basil.

Makes 4 servings.

Each serving contains:

Cal	Prot	Carb	Fib	Tot. Fat	Sat. Fat	Chol	Sodium
218	5g	26g	4g	11g	2g	0mg	228mg

ARUGULA-POTATO SOUP

Arugula adds distinction to simple potato soup, transforming it into a dish with great character. It is a matter of personal preference whether or not to peel the potatoes. Unless the skins are very thick, I leave them on for added flavor and texture.

5 cups (1.25 liters) vegetable
 stock or water
2 tablespoons olive oil
2 cloves garlic, chopped
1/2 lb. (225g) potatoes, cubed
4 oz. (115g) arugula

1/4 cup chopped parsley leaves
Salt and pepper to taste
Extra-virgin olive oil (optional)
Freshly grated pecorino or
 Parmesan cheese

1. Bring stock or water to a boil.
2. Heat oil in a large saucepan. Add garlic and cook gently until fragrant. Add potatoes and stir 2 to 3 minutes. Add arugula and parsley and mix well. Add boiling stock or water, return to a boil and simmer, partially covered, until potatoes are tender.
3. Season with salt and pepper.
4. Serve with a little olive oil swirled through, if desired, and grated cheese sprinkled on top.

Makes 4 servings.

Each serving contains:

Cal	Prot	Carb	Fib	Tot. Fat	Sat. Fat	Chol	Sodium
183	6g	22g	3g	9g	2g	5mg	210mg

PASTA AND CHICKPEA SOUP

Thick, warming and as garlicky as you like, this is a wonderful cool-weather snack or lunch. To give it more character, swirl extra-virgin olive oil into each bowlful. The flavor of the oil will vary according to where the olives were grown. For example, a Tuscan oil has a full-bodied, peppery taste while one from farther south is more delicate.

2 tablespoons virgin olive oil
1 onion, chopped
1-3 cloves garlic, chopped
2 large tomatoes, chopped
1 teaspoon chopped fresh
  rosemary leaves
1 can (14-oz. / 400g) chickpeas,
  drained

2 cups (500ml) vegetable or
  chicken stock or water
5 oz. (145g) macaroni
Salt and pepper to taste
Freshly grated Parmesan cheese

1. Heat oil in a saucepan. Sauté onion and garlic until softened.
2. Coarsely purée tomatoes, rosemary, half the chickpeas and half the stock or water in a food processor or blender.
3. Stir puréed ingredients into the saucepan and bring to a boil. Cover and simmer gently 5 minutes.
4. Bring remaining stock or water to a boil and add to the pan. Add macaroni, stir, cover and simmer until macaroni is tender. Add more boiling stock or water if necessary to maintain a soupy consistency.
5. Add remaining chickpeas, salt and pepper and heat through. Serve with grated cheese on top.

Makes 4 servings.

Each serving contains:

Cal	Prot	Carb	Fib	Tot. Fat	Sat. Fat	Chol	Sodium
359	13g	53g	9g	11g	2g	5mg	415mg

FIGS WITH PARMA HAM

Melon and Parma ham have been eaten together for a long time, but I think black figs make a more exciting accompaniment.

1/2 cup (125ml) olive oil
2 tablespoons white-wine vinegar
Salt and pepper to taste

3 ripe black figs, quartered
12 thin slices of Parma ham
Mascarpone cheese (optional)

1. Whisk together oil, vinegar, salt and pepper; toss with figs.
2. Lay out ham slices and fold them lengthwise. Place a fig quarter on one end of each piece of ham and roll up. Serve with a little mascarpone cheese, if desired.

Makes 4 servings.

Each serving contains:

Cal	Prot	Carb	Fib	Tot. Fat	Sat. Fat	Chol	Sodium
413	11g	8g	1g	38g	7g	32mg	931mg

EGGPLANT-MOZZARELLA ROLLS

Broiled eggplant slices combine readily with mozzarella cheese, and I have devised several ways to vary the partnership. When I have time and am cooking for more than two people, I often make all of these variations and serve a large eggplant-and-mozzarella platter.

1 eggplant, about 12 oz. (340g)   *4 oz. (115g) mozzarella cheese*
Freshly ground black pepper   *8 basil leaves*
Virgin olive oil   *Salt to taste*

1. Preheat broiler. Cut eggplant lengthwise into 8 slices. Season with pepper and brush with oil. Broil until tender and browned on one side but only lightly colored on the other.
2. Cut cheese into 8 slices.
3. Lay a cheese slice on browned side of each eggplant slice, top with a basil leaf and roll up. Return to broiler, seam side down, until cheese softens. Sprinkle with salt and serve immediately.

Makes 2 to 4 servings.

Variations

1. Eggplant-Mozzarella Sandwiches—Broil thin eggplant slices and sandwich them together with thinly sliced mozzarella. Top with finely chopped anchovies, capers and parsley and broil until cheese softens.
2. Pizza-Style Eggplant Slices—Spread broiled eggplant slices with a little tomato sauce or paste. Cover with mozzarella slices, top with chopped anchovies and return to the broiler until cheese bubbles.

Each serving contains:

Cal	Prot	Carb	Fib	Tot. Fat	Sat. Fat	Chol	Sodium
323	12g	12g	4g	26g	9g	44mg	350mg

EGGPLANTS WITH PESTO SAUCE

I love the soft, silky texture and smoky taste of broiled eggplant, and the wonderful heady taste of pesto sauce, so it is hardly surprising this dish is a long-standing favorite of mine. Save time by using a good commercial pesto sauce.

2 small eggplants, 8 oz. (225g) each

PESTO
2 cloves garlic
2 tablespoons pine nuts
1/2 oz. (15g) basil leaves

6 tablespoons (90ml) virgin olive
oil, plus extra for brushing
3 tablespoons mixed grated
pecorino and Parmesan cheese,
or all Parmesan cheese
Pepper to taste

1. Preheat broiler.
2. Cut eggplants in half lengthwise, then score flesh deeply in a diamond pattern. Be careful not to pierce the skin. Brush with oil, then broil, cut side up first, until tender and browned.
3. Make pesto: Drop garlic into a blender or food processor with motor running, then add pine nuts, basil leaves and oil. Mix until smooth and add cheese. Mix very briefly. Season with pepper.
4. Spread pesto over cut side of eggplants and return to broiler until pesto begins to bubble.

Makes 4 servings.

Each serving contains:

Cal	Prot	Carb	Fib	Tot. Fat	Sat. Fat	Chol	Sodium
331	4g	9g	4g	33g	5g	4mg	96mg

EGGPLANT, TOMATOES AND MOZZARELLA

The aroma of this simple dish will give a boost to jaded taste buds, and its savory taste will perk up any flagging appetite.

8 oz. (225g) eggplant, sliced
3 tablespoons virgin olive oil
Finely grated zest of 1 lemon
Salt and pepper to taste
5 oz. (145g) mozzarella cheese,
* thinly sliced*

1 lb. (450g) tomatoes, thinly
* sliced*
4 tablespoons torn basil leaves
Warm Italian bread

1. Preheat broiler. Brush eggplant slices lightly with oil. Place in a single layer on broiler rack and broil until golden on both sides.
2. Whisk together remaining oil, lemon zest, salt and pepper.
3. Arrange eggplant, cheese and tomatoes in a single layer of over-lapping slices in a large shallow baking dish. Pour dressing over.
4. Broil 3 to 4 minutes until cheese begins to melt. Sprinkle with basil leaves and serve immediately with warm bread.

Makes 4 servings.

Each serving contains:

Cal	Prot	Carb	Fib	Tot. Fat	Sat. Fat	Chol	Sodium
320	11g	26g	3g	20g	6g	29mg	374mg

RADICCHIO WITH GOAT CHEESE

You could omit making a hollow in the radicchio halves and sprinkle the broiled radicchio with freshly grated Parmesan cheese, which should begin to melt just from the heat of the leaves. Or sprinkle the broiled halves with grated fontina or mozzarella cheese and return to the broiler until the cheese melts.

2 heads of radicchio, halved
4 tablespoons extra-virgin
   olive oil
Salt and pepper to taste

4 slices of fresh goat cheese,
   about 1/4 inch (6mm) thick
Leaves from 2-3 sprigs of thyme

1. Preheat broiler. Remove a few leaves from the center of each radicchio half and reserve for a salad or snack. Brush radicchio halves with oil. Season with salt and pepper. Broil until edges brown.
2. Put 1 cheese slice in the hollow of each piece of radicchio, brush with oil and sprinkle with thyme. Return to broiler until cheese begins to bubble. Sprinkle with more pepper and serve.

Makes 4 servings.

Each serving contains:

Cal	Prot	Carb	Fib	Tot. Fat	Sat. Fat	Chol	Sodium
232	7g	3g	0g	22g	8g	22mg	221mg

SWEET-AND-SOUR ONIONS

The onions used in Italy for this dish are sold in bunches, like green onions. I have made this recipe using very fat green onions. They take less time to cook and don't have to be peeled. Another way to save time is to use frozen pearl onions; there is no need to thaw them.

3/4 lb. (340g) frozen small whole onions
2 tablespoons olive oil
2 tablespoons balsamic vinegar

1 bay leaf, torn
Pinch of brown sugar
Pepper to taste

1. Simmer onions in salted water about 5 minutes. Drain well.
2. Heat oil in a heavy skillet large enough to hold the onions in a single layer. Add onions and sauté, turning them occasionally, until browned.
3. Add vinegar, bay leaf, sugar and pepper. Cook and stir until onions are coated with a slightly syrupy sauce. Discard bay leaf.
4. Serve warm.

Makes 4 servings.

Each serving contains:

Cal	Prot	Carb	Fib	Tot. Fat	Sat. Fat	Chol	Sodium
100	1g	9g	1g	7g	1g	0mg	199mg

STUFFED MUSHROOMS

The filling can be flavored with anchovy paste or chopped anchovy fillets—in which case, halve the amount of cheese. If it is more convenient, the mushrooms can be cooked under a moderate broiler.

4 large fresh mushrooms
1 small tomato, seeded and
  chopped
4 tablespoons freshly grated
  Parmesan cheese
3 tablespoons fresh breadcrumbs

1 egg, beaten
1 clove garlic, finely chopped
1 tablespoon chopped parsley
1 tablespoon virgin olive oil
Salt and pepper to taste

1. Preheat oven to 425F (220C). Oil a shallow baking dish.
2. Remove and chop mushroom stems. Mix with tomato, cheese, breadcrumbs, egg, garlic, parsley, 1 teaspoon oil, salt and pepper.
3. Put mushroom caps in baking dish, open side up, fill with breadcrumb mixture and drizzle with remaining oil. Bake 15 minutes until mushrooms are cooked as desired and tops are brown.

Makes 4 servings.

Each serving contains:

Cal	Prot	Carb	Fib	Tot. Fat	Sat. Fat	Chol	Sodium
98	5g	5g	1g	6g	2g	58mg	212mg

BAGNA CAUDA

Bagna cauda is a rich, pungent, anchovy-and-garlic sauce or dip from Piedmont. Raw or lightly cooked vegetables are served for dipping in the bagna cauda—in season, cardoon is traditional. The sauce is also good spooned over halved hard-cooked eggs.

When only a small amount of sauce is left, eggs are added to it and scrambled. Leftover bagna cauda (without the scrambled eggs) is good with pasta. Butter and oil proportions can be altered to taste, and cream is sometimes used to mute the pungency.

*1 can (2-oz. / 60g) anchovy fillets
  in oil
4 cloves garlic, finely chopped
2/3 cup (160ml) olive oil
6 tablespoons (85g) unsalted
  butter, diced*

*Pepper to taste
Raw or blanched vegetables or
  halved hard-cooked eggs
Thickly sliced Italian bread*

1. Drain oil from anchovies into a saucepan. Chop anchovies and add to pan with garlic and olive oil. Heat gently, mashing anchovies until they dissolve; cook until garlic has softened and begins to color.
2. Stir in butter and pepper. Pour into a small fondue pot or other small pot to put over heat when serving.
3. Use long forks to dip vegetables into sauce, stirring to keep well mixed. Or spoon sauce over hard-cooked eggs.
4. Serve with thick slices of bread.

Makes 4 to 6 servings.

Each serving of sauce contains:

Cal	Prot	Carb	Fib	Tot. Fat	Sat. Fat	Chol	Sodium
505	4g	1g	0g	55g	16g	59mg	523mg

MOZZARELLA FRITTERS *fair - do not overcook!*

Cornmeal gives a crisp, crunchy coating. To add extra flavor, spread a little pesto on the cheese slices or mix some finely chopped herbs into the cornmeal. Frying the fritters quickly ensures that they come out crisp and dry. Serve as a snack, or with a crisp salad for a light main course.

1 egg, beaten
Salt and pepper to taste
2 mozzarella cheeses, each about
  5 oz. (145g)

1/2 cup (60g) fine cornmeal
Olive oil for deep frying

1. Season egg with salt and pepper. Cut cheese into slices 1/2 inch (1.25cm) thick. Dip in egg, then coat lightly and evenly with cornmeal.
2. Fill a deep-fat fryer or a deep skillet two-thirds full with oil and heat to 350F (180C). Add cheese slices and fry 2 to 3 minutes until crisp and lightly browned.
3. Remove slices and drain quickly on paper towels. Serve immediately.

Makes 4 servings.

Each serving contains:

Cal	Prot	Carb	Fib	Tot. Fat	Sat. Fat	Chol	Sodium
400	17g	15g	2g	30g	16g	108mg	347mg

MOZZARELLA IN CARROZZA

There are no exotic ingredients in this classic Neapolitan dish. But if it is as it should be—light and crisp on the outside, with delicious, just-melting cheese that pulls into strings on the inside—it is far from ordinary. Serve as a snack, a first course or with a crisp salad for lunch.

Olive oil for deep-frying
5 oz. (145g) buffalo mozzarella
  cheese
8 thin slices of white bread, crusts
  removed, cut in half

7 tablespoons (100ml) milk
Freshly ground black pepper
6 tablespoons all-purpose flour
2 eggs, beaten

1. Half-fill deep-fat fryer or skillet with oil and heat to 350F (180C).
2. Cut cheese into 8 slices the same size as the bread.
3. Quickly dip one side of a piece of bread in milk, then place a cheese slice on the dry side. Grind pepper over.
4. Dip one side of another bread piece in milk and place on the cheese, dry side down. Dust the "sandwich" with flour, then dip in egg. Allow excess egg to drain off. Repeat with remaining bread and cheese.
5. Fry sandwiches in batches until golden and crisp on both sides. Using a slotted spoon, transfer to paper towels to drain.

Makes 4 servings.

Variations
1. Top cheese with chopped herbs, sliced black olives, sun-dried tomatoes or chopped anchovy fillets.
2. Spread cheese with pesto, sun-dried-tomato paste, black-olive paste or anchovy paste.

Each serving contains:

Cal	Prot	Carb	Fib	Tot. Fat	Sat. Fat	Chol	Sodium
494	18g	45g	2g	27g	8g	139mg	503mg

VENETIAN SHRIMP AND BEANS

I first ate this dish in Venice, made with the local specialty, *gamberetti*—fresh tiny, sweet shrimp. I have since had it a number of times all along the Adriatic coast. If fresh shrimp are not available, use fresh, juicy prawns or crayfish. The dish can also be a main course.

1 small carrot
1 small stalk celery
1 slice lemon
1-1/4 lb. (575g) fresh shrimp or prawns in their shells
1 can (14-oz. / 400g) cannellini beans, drained

2 tomatoes, chopped
1 clove garlic, chopped (optional)
3 tablespoons virgin olive oil
1 tablespoon lemon juice
Salt and pepper to taste
2-1/2 tablespoons chopped basil or a few torn arugula leaves

1. Add carrot, celery and lemon slice to a saucepan of water and bring to a boil. Add shrimp or prawns, cover and quickly return to a boil. Boil 2 to 4 minutes until cooked.
2. Put beans into a saucepan, cover with water and heat through.
3. Combine tomatoes, garlic, if using, olive oil, lemon juice, salt and pepper.
4. Drain shrimp or prawns, rinse under running cold water and peel. Cut large prawns into bite-size pieces.
5. Drain beans and toss with shrimp or prawns, tomatoes and basil or arugula. Let stand 15 to 45 minutes.

Makes 4 servings.

Each serving contains:

Cal	Prot	Carb	Fib	Tot. Fat	Sat. Fat	Chol	Sodium
292	26g	19g	5g	12g	2g	202mg	526mg

BRUSCHETTA SUPREME

The original Roman *bruschetta* was bread toasted over a charcoal fire, then rubbed with a cut garlic clove and sprinkled with olive oil. Halved or chopped juicy tomatoes pressed into the bread before the oil was added made a simple variation, *bruschetta al pomodoro*. Today there are many ways to prepare bruschetta. This one bursts with so much flavor that no one would ever guess it had been made at a moment's notice.

1 tablespoon capers, drained
6 sun-dried tomato halves, packed in oil
10-12 oil-cured black olives, pitted
6 tablespoons coarsely chopped parsley
1 red onion, thinly sliced

1 tablespoon oil from the sun-dried tomatoes
5 tablespoons extra-virgin olive oil
Pepper to taste
4 slices of firm well-flavored Italian or French bread

1. Preheat broiler. Coarsely chop capers, sun-dried tomatoes and olives and mix together. Toss with parsley, onion, oil from the sun-dried tomatoes, olive oil and pepper.
2. Toast bread on both sides. Pile topping on bread and serve.

Makes 4 servings.

Each serving contains:

Cal	Prot	Carb	Fib	Tot. Fat	Sat. Fat	Chol	Sodium
297	3g	19g	3g	23g	3g	0mg	384mg

PARMESAN BRUSCHETTA

This recipe is really the Italian version of cheese on toast and is so simple it hardly needs a recipe.

4 slices of firm, well-flavored
   Italian bread, such as ciabatta
   or pugliese
1 clove garlic, halved
2-3 tablespoons extra-virgin
   olive oil

3/4 cup (85g) freshly grated
   Parmesan cheese
Freshly ground black pepper

1. Preheat broiler. Toast bread until lightly browned on both sides.
2. Rub cut side of garlic over one side of each slice of bread. Brush bread with olive oil and sprinkle with cheese.
3. Return to broiler for 1 minute until cheese begins to melt. Grind pepper over cheese and serve immediately.

Makes 4 servings.

Each serving contains:

Cal	Prot	Carb	Fib	Tot. Fat	Sat. Fat	Chol	Sodium
258	10g	16g	1g	17g	5g	15mg	521mg

ZUCCHINI PIZZA ROLLS

I love good pizza and although an Italian would not class these rolls as pizzas, they are good. They also have the advantage of being cooked quickly under the broiler instead of in the oven.

4 tablespoons tomato paste
7 tablespoons pesto
Virgin olive oil
1 clove garlic, crushed
Salt and pepper to taste
4 Italian rolls or hamburger buns,
* halved*

1/2 lb. (225g) small zucchini,
* thinly sliced on diagonal*
3-1/2 oz. (100g) mozzarella
* cheese, thinly sliced*
Small handful of basil leaves, torn

1. Preheat broiler. Combine tomato paste, pesto, 1 tablespoon olive oil, garlic, salt and pepper, and spread over cut sides of rolls.
2. Arrange zucchini in overlapping circles on rolls. Brush with olive oil, season with pepper and put under broiler about 5 minutes until beginning to soften.
3. Place cheese slices on zucchini. Return to broiler until cheese bubbles.
4. Top with basil and more pepper.

Makes 4 servings.

Each serving contains:

Cal	Prot	Carb	Fib	Tot. Fat	Sat. Fat	Chol	Sodium
399	13g	22g	3g	29g	8g	27mg	650mg

BEANS ON GARLIC TOAST

I love these beans on toast for a quick and satisfying snack. I also serve them, without toast, as an accompaniment to broiled or fried meat or sausages, using just 2 slices of pancetta or bacon. You can substitute 2 tablespoons chopped rosemary for the thyme or parsley.

Virgin olive oil
1 red onion, chopped
2 cloves garlic, crushed
4 slices of pancetta or bacon,
  chopped
1 tablespoon chopped thyme or
  parsley (optional)

4 slices firm bread
1 can (14 oz. / 400g) cannellini
  or borlotti beans, rinsed and
  drained
Salt and pepper to taste

1. Preheat broiler.
2. Heat 2 tablespoons olive oil in skillet; add onion, 1 crushed garlic clove and pancetta or bacon. Sauté 3 to 4 minutes, adding thyme or parsley, if used, toward the end.
3. When broiler is hot, toast bread on one side. Rub the other side with remaining garlic, then brush with olive oil and broil.
4. Add beans, salt and pepper to onion mixture and heat through. Spoon onto toast and serve.

Makes 4 servings.

Each serving contains:

Cal	Prot	Carb	Fib	Tot. Fat	Sat. Fat	Chol	Sodium
370	13g	32g	5g	21g	5g	16mg	754mg

POACHED EGGS AND CHEESE

Fontina cheese is made from the milk of cows that graze on the lush herb-and-flower-strewn summer pastures of the Alps, so it is not surprising the cheese has a distinctive sweet flavor. It has a semisoft texture and melts nicely when heated. In the original Piedmontese dish the bread and eggs are fried, but I prefer toasting and poaching them respectively.

4 slices firm bread
4 eggs
4 slices fontina cheese
4 anchovy fillets, chopped

2 tablespoons (30g) butter, diced
Freshly ground black pepper
Chopped parsley

1. Preheat broiler.
2. Toast one side of each slice of bread.
3. Bring a skillet of water to simmering point. Carefully break eggs into it and poach for about 3 minutes or until set as desired. Spoon hot water over eggs while cooking.
4. Place cheese slices on untoasted sides of bread and put under broiler until melted. Turn off broiler. Use half of chopped anchovies to top cheese slices; place under broiler to heat.
5. Melt butter in a small pan, add remaining anchovies and mash until dissolved. Season with pepper.
6. Put an egg on each slice of bread and top with anchovy sauce. Sprinkle with chopped parsley.

Makes 4 servings.

Each serving contains:

Cal	Prot	Carb	Fib	Tot. Fat	Sat. Fat	Chol	Sodium
298	16g	16g	1g	19g	10g	256mg	615mg

BEAN-CHEESE FRITTATA

I prefer to leave a frittata slightly moist, but you can set its top by putting the pan under the broiler.

6 oz. (170g) shelled fresh young
  fava or lima beans or thawed
  frozen beans
Salt to taste
4 eggs

2 teaspoons finely chopped dill
Pepper to taste
1 tablespoon (15g) unsalted
  butter
2-1/2 oz. (70g) goat cheese, grated

1. Cook beans in boiling salted water until tender. Drain well.
2. Lightly beat eggs with dill, salt and pepper until yolks and whites are blended. Stir in beans.
3. In a heavy skillet, 8 or 9 inches (20-22.5cm) in diameter, heat butter until foamy. Pour in egg mixture, turn heat to very low and cook about 15 minutes until eggs are set but top is still creamy. Sprinkle with cheese.
4. If desired, put pan under preheated broiler to set the top of the frittata. Serve immediately with a side salad and crusty bread.

Makes 2 servings.

Each serving contains:

Cal	Prot	Carb	Fib	Tot. Fat	Sat. Fat	Chol	Sodium
456	29g	19g	4g	29g	16g	478mg	390mg

Frittatas ~ *A frittata, usually described as an Italian omelet, is quite unlike the classic French omelet. Frittatas are thick, the filling is contained within the egg mixture, they are cooked slowly, and they are often cut into wedges for serving. They are naturals for all manner of fillings—chopped sausages, cured meats, chicken, fish and shellfish, vegetables, cheese, herbs or pantry ingredients such as sun-dried tomatoes, capers or anchovy fillets.*

ZUCCHINI FRITTATA

It is important to use small zucchini; not only will they have the best flavor but they will be firm and will not exude a lot of moisture when cooked. If you have only large zucchini, slice, grate or chop them as directed, then sprinkle with salt and set aside for about 20 minutes. Rinse well and pat dry before using.

1 tablespoon olive oil
1/2 lb. (225g) small zucchini,
  coarsely grated
4 eggs
3 tablespoons freshly grated
  Parmesan cheese

1 tablespoon chopped parsley
1 tablespoon chopped basil
Salt and pepper to taste
1 tablespoon (15g) unsalted butter

1. Heat oil in a heavy skillet 8 or 9 inches (20-22.5cm) in diameter. Add zucchini and sauté until light brown.
2. Lightly beat together eggs, cheese, herbs, salt and pepper until yolks and whites are blended.
3. If the zucchini have produced a lot of moisture, raise the heat and boil it off. Add butter. When it is foamy, turn heat to very low and stir in egg mixture. Cook about 15 minutes until eggs are set but top is still creamy.
4. If desired, put the pan under a preheated broiler to set the top of the frittata.

Makes 2 servings.

Each serving contains:

Cal	Prot	Carb	Fib	Tot. Fat	Sat. Fat	Chol	Sodium
318	18g	5g	1g	25g	9g	448mg	438mg

BASIL FRITTATA

This is a simple yet flavorful frittata. When fresh basil is really fragrant, I think it is my favorite.

6 eggs
3 tablespoons freshly grated
* Parmesan cheese*

4 tablespoons torn basil leaves
Salt and pepper to taste
3 tablespoons (45g) unsalted butter

1. Lightly beat eggs with cheese, basil, salt and pepper until yolks and whites are blended.
2. In a heavy skillet, 10 inches (25cm) in diameter, heat butter over moderate heat until foamy. Pour in egg mixture, turn heat to very low and cook about 15 minutes until eggs are set but top is still creamy.
3. If desired, put pan under preheated broiler to set top of frittata.

Makes 4 servings.

Each serving contains:

Cal	Prot	Carb	Fib	Tot. Fat	Sat. Fat	Chol	Sodium
209	11g	1g	0g	18g	9g	346mg	250mg

ASPARAGUS WITH EGGS AND CHEESE

Traditionally, cooked asparagus spears are dipped in butter, egg yolk and Parmesan cheese. The eggs can be fried, poached or soft-boiled but the yolks must be soft—you can't dip an asparagus tip into a hard yolk! Italians use fat, white asparagus but I think slim, green spears are better for this recipe—and they cook more quickly.

Salt

10 oz. (280g) asparagus spears

2 eggs

1 tablespoon (15g) unsalted
   butter, melted

Freshly grated Parmesan cheese

Freshly grated black pepper

1. Bring a tall saucepan of salted water to a boil. Divide asparagus into two bundles and tie at the bottom and beneath the tips. Place in pan and cover with lid or foil. Boil 10 to 15 minutes.
2. Cook eggs as desired, making sure to keep yolks soft.
3. Remove asparagus from water, untie bundles and spread spears out between two thick layers of paper towels.
4. Arrange asparagus and eggs on 2 warm plates. Pour butter over asparagus tips. Sprinkle with Parmesan and pepper. Dip pieces of asparagus into egg yolk as you eat.

Makes 2 servings.

Each serving contains:

Cal	Prot	Carb	Fib	Tot. Fat	Sat. Fat	Chol	Sodium
215	15g	8g	3g	15g	8g	238mg	299mg

EGGS AND BASIL IN HAM PARCELS

This is an Italian version of the ever-popular combination of ham and eggs. Convention says the eggs should be placed cut side down, but I think the parcels are nicer to eat if the yolks are uppermost.

4 large eggs, at room temperature *Extra-virgin olive oil*
12 small basil leaves *Freshly ground black pepper*
8 thin slices of Parma ham

1. Bring water to a boil in a saucepan large enough to hold the eggs. Using a spoon, carefully lower eggs into water. Simmer 6 to 7 minutes for soft yolks, 10 to 12 minutes for firm yolks.
2. Drain eggs and rinse under cold running water. Peel and cut in half lengthwise. Tear one basil leaf over each half and season with pepper. Wrap in a slice of Parma ham. Drizzle olive oil over the top. Tear remaining basil leaves and sprinkle them over the egg parcels.

Makes 4 servings.

Each serving contains:

Cal	Prot	Carb	Fib	Tot. Fat	Sat. Fat	Chol	Sodium
221	18g	1g	0g	16g	4g	240mg	790mg

EGGS WITH TUNA SAUCE

Tuna sauce is so quick and delicious it is a shame to restrict its use to the traditional *Vitello tonnato* (cold poached veal with tuna sauce). The sauce goes equally well with boiled eggs, making a dish that is practical and economical. If the quantity of sauce is too much for four eggs, keep the remainder in a covered container in the refrigerator for two days and use as a dip for crudités or as a pasta sauce.

4 large eggs, at room temperature
1 can (7-oz. / 200g) tuna, packed
  in olive oil
4 anchovy fillets
1/2 cup (125ml) mayonnaise
2 tablespoons capers, drained

2 tablespoons lemon juice
Freshly ground black pepper
Crisp lettuce leaves
Chopped parsley
Italian or French bread

1. Bring water to a boil in a saucepan large enough to hold the eggs. Using a spoon, carefully lower eggs into water. Simmer 6 to 7 minutes for soft yolks, 10 to 12 minutes for firm yolks.
2. Put tuna and its oil, anchovies, mayonnaise and capers in a blender or food processor. Mix until smooth, then add lemon juice and pepper to taste. Make a small bed of leaves on each of 4 plates.
3. Drain eggs and rinse under running cold water. Peel them and cut in half lengthwise. Put 2 or 3 halves, cut side down, on each plate. Top with sauce and parsley.
4. Serve with Italian or French bread.

Makes 4 servings.

Each serving contains:

Cal	Prot	Carb	Fib	Tot. Fat	Sat. Fat	Chol	Sodium
486	24g	17g	1g	36g	6g	248mg	896mg

Chapter Two

VEGETABLES AND SALADS

Vegetables play an important part in the Italian diet. Not only do they accompany the meat, fish or poultry, but a vegetable dish may actually be the main course. No matter how simple the recipe—Zucchini with Oregano, for example—it always tastes good. This is because Italians buy vegetables in peak condition, full of flavor and very fresh, and they know how to use them to their best advantage.

The secrets of good cooking can be passed on, but unless produce of a similar quality is used, it is impossible to create dishes that taste as wonderful as they do in Italy.

With the greatly expanded range of salad greens and flavoring ingredients now available, it is possible to make exciting and varied Italian-style salads. Some are suitable accompaniments to main courses, some make good first courses and others are ideal for a light meal, perhaps preceded by a soup and served with firm bread.

BROILED ARTICHOKE SALAD

Large artichoke hearts preserved in oil can be bought loose from Italian food shops and delicatessens. Or you can use bottled artichoke hearts in oil. If you do, some of the oil can be used for this salad and the remainder kept for other salads or for tossing with pasta. Do not use artichokes in brine.

8 large artichokes preserved in oil
4 Little Gem lettuces or lettuce
  hearts
1 tablespoon lemon juice

5 tablespoons olive oil or oil from
  the artichokes
Salt and pepper to taste

1. Preheat broiler. Cut artichokes in half from top to bottom. Lay artichoke halves on broiler rack and brown under the broiler.
2. Divide lettuces into leaves and arrange on serving plate. Whisk together lemon juice, oil, salt and pepper and spoon over lettuce.
3. Place artichoke hearts on top.

Makes 4 servings.

Each serving contains:

Cal	Prot	Carb	Fib	Tot. Fat	Sat. Fat	Chol	Sodium
202	4g	9g	2g	17g	2g	0mg	316mg

TUSCAN BREAD SALAD

Panzanella is a classic bread salad from Tuscany. Its success lies in the quality of the bread and really flavorful tomatoes. This version uses sun-dried tomatoes and the oil in which they have been packed. Capers may also be added.

4 slices Italian bread
12 sun-dried tomato halves, packed in oil
A handful of arugula or young spinach leaves
8 oil-cured black olives, halved, pitted

5 tablespoons oil from the sun-dried tomatoes
1 tablespoon red-wine vinegar
Salt and pepper to taste

1. Soak bread in cold water 5 to 10 minutes.
2. Chop sun-dried tomatoes. Tear arugula or spinach leaves into a salad bowl.
3. Drain bread and squeeze out as much water as possible. Tear bread into pieces. Add to bowl, scatter olives and tomatoes over and mix everything together.
4. Using a fork, whisk together oil from sun-dried tomatoes, vinegar, salt and pepper, pour over salad and toss to mix well; if salad is too dry, add more oil.

Makes 2 servings.

Each serving contains:

Cal	Prot	Carb	Fib	Tot. Fat	Sat. Fat	Chol	Sodium
524	6g	36g	4g	40g	6g	0mg	688mg

MUSHROOM-PARMESAN SALAD

Some people like to serve this salad as soon as it has been made while others prefer to leave it for a while. For me, it depends on how I feel and the amount of time available.

10 oz. (280g) porcini (cep),
   oyster or other large
   mushrooms, thinly sliced
2-1/2-oz. (70g) piece Parmesan
   cheese

10 basil leaves, torn
3 tablespoons virgin olive oil
1 tablespoon lemon juice
Salt and pepper to taste

1. Arrange mushrooms on a large serving plate. Using a potato peeler, shave strips of Parmesan cheese over mushrooms. Scatter basil over cheese.
2. Using a fork, whisk together oil, lemon juice, salt and pepper. Pour over salad. Serve at once or leave for up to 30 minutes.

Makes 4 servings.

Each serving contains:

Cal	Prot	Carb	Fib	Tot. Fat	Sat. Fat	Chol	Sodium
188	9g	4g	1g	16g	5g	14mg	399mg

WARM MUSHROOM-PANCETTA SALAD

No pancetta? Use thick-cut smoked bacon. No balsamic vinegar? Substitute 3/4 tablespoon tarragon vinegar for both vinegars. Serve as a first course or as an accompaniment to Rosemary-Lemon Chicken, page 91, or Pork with Sage, page 100.

3 oz. (85g) pancetta or bacon, cut into strips
1 clove garlic
Salt to taste
3/4 lb. (340g) oyster or brown cap mushrooms
3 tablespoons virgin olive oil
Pepper to taste
Mixed salad greens
Chopped tarragon, chervil, basil or parsley (optional)
1/2 tablespoon balsamic vinegar
1/2 tablespoon white-wine vinegar

1. Heat a heavy skillet, add pancetta or bacon and cook until crisp.
2. Crush garlic with a pinch of salt, then chop it. Break mushrooms into pieces.
3. Using a slotted spoon, transfer pancetta or bacon to paper towels. Add oil, garlic, mushrooms, salt and pepper to pan and cook 3 to 4 minutes until just tender.
4. Divide salad greens among 4 plates.
5. Quickly tip pancetta and herbs, if using, onto mushrooms. Using a slotted spoon, lift from pan and scatter over greens.
6. Stir vinegars into skillet and boil 1 to 2 minutes. Pour over salads and serve immediately.

Makes 4 servings.

Each serving contains:

Cal	Prot	Carb	Fib	Tot. Fat	Sat. Fat	Chol	Sodium
141	5g	5g	2g	12g	2g	8mg	277mg

FENNEL-RICOTTA SALAD

The crisp anise flavor of fennel marries well with the delicate taste of ricotta cheese. Serve this as a first course.

1 lb. (450g) small fennel bulbs	6 tablespoons (90ml) virgin
1/2 clove garlic	olive oil
Salt to taste	Pepper to taste
2 tablespoons lemon juice	4 oz. (115g) ricotta cheese

1. Very thinly slice fennel bulbs; reserve green fronds. Put fennel in a shallow serving dish.
2. Crush garlic with a pinch of salt, then whisk with lemon juice, oil and pepper. Pour over fennel.
3. Break up ricotta cheese with a fork and spoon onto fennel. Toss lightly. Snip reserved fronds over the salad.

Makes 4 servings.

Variation

Fennel-Gorgonzola Salad—Substitute Gorgonzola cheese for the ricotta and sprinkle chopped walnuts over the salad.

Each serving contains:

Cal	Prot	Carb	Fib	Tot. Fat	Sat. Fat	Chol	Sodium
263	5g	9g	5g	24g	5g	14mg	149mg

ZUCCHINI-PARMESAN SALAD

This beautifully light, fresh-tasting salad is one of my summertime favorites. Add a few mint or parsley leaves for more flavor.

1/2 lb. (225g) small zucchini
2-oz. (60g) piece Parmesan
   cheese
3 tablespoons lemon juice

5 tablespoons extra-virgin or
   virgin olive oil
Salt to taste

1. Slice zucchini very thinly. Arrange slices on a serving plate so that they overlap slightly.
2. Using a potato peeler, shave Parmesan into thin slivers and scatter over zucchini.
3. Whisk together lemon juice, oil, salt and pepper. Pour over cheese and zucchini. Serve immediately.

Makes 2 servings.

Each serving contains:

Cal	Prot	Carb	Fib	Tot. Fat	Sat. Fat	Chol	Sodium
444	14g	4g	2g	42g	10g	22mg	664mg

WARM ARUGULA AND POTATO SALAD

For the cheese you can use taleggio, which is a mild, creamy, young cheese from northern Italy, a buttery Gorgonzola (but not a strong, piquant one) or a creamy Dolcelatte. If you do not have arugula, use young spinach leaves.

3/4 lb. (340g) small new potatoes
Salt
6 oz. (170g) mild Italian blue
  cheese
Large handful of arugula or
  spinach leaves

1 tablespoon hazelnut oil or
  walnut oil
1 tablespoon extra-virgin olive oil
Freshly ground black pepper

1. Cook potatoes in boiling salted water until tender.
2. Coarsely chop cheese. Tear arugula or spinach into large pieces and place in 2 or 3 individual salad bowls.
3. Drain potatoes, quickly cut them in half and add to the salad bowls. Scatter cheese over potatoes, sprinkle oils over and toss everything together. Grind pepper over salads and serve.

Makes 3 servings.

Each serving contains:

Cal	Prot	Carb	Fib	Tot. Fat	Sat. Fat	Chol	Sodium
367	14g	22g	1g	25g	12g	43mg	886mg

ARUGULA, TOMATO AND MOZZARELLA SALAD

The distinctive flavor of arugula marries well with the sweet juiciness of the tomatoes and the mild creaminess of mozzarella. The result a sophisticated but simple-tasting salad. Little Gem lettuce or radicchio can be used instead of arugula.

Arugula leaves
5 oz. (145g) mozzarella cheese, chopped
8 cherry tomatoes, halved

Freshly ground black pepper
3 tablespoons virgin olive oil
1 tablespoon white-wine vinegar
Salt to taste

1. Divide arugula between 2 plates. Scatter cheese and tomatoes over it. Coarsely grind pepper on top.
2. Using a fork, whisk together oil, vinegar and salt. Pour dressing over salads and toss to mix.

Makes 2 servings.

Each serving contains:

Cal	Prot	Carb	Fib	Tot. Fat	Sat. Fat	Chol	Sodium
396	14g	5g	1g	36g	12g	56mg	405mg

TOMATO, MOZZARELLA AND BASIL SALAD

In concept this is the hackneyed and abused *salade Caprese* of Italian restaurants. But, when you have really well-flavored tomatoes and genuine buffalo mozzarella, it is a rare treat—and so quick and simple!

5oz. (145g) buffalo mozzarella cheese, thinly sliced
1 lb. (450g) very ripe tomatoes, thinly sliced

15 basil leaves
Salt and pepper to taste
2-3 tablespoons extra-virgin olive oil

1. Arrange cheese and tomatoes on 4 plates so they overlap.
2. Scatter basil leaves over them, sprinkle with salt and pepper and trickle with oil.

Makes 4 servings.

Each serving contains:

Cal	Prot	Carb	Fib	Tot. Fat	Sat. Fat	Chol	Sodium
213	8g	6g	1g	18g	6g	28mg	209mg

BEAN AND TUNA SALAD

Fagioli e tonnato (bean and tuna salad) is one of the classic antipasto dishes. The additions to the basic recipe are many and varied—black olives, chopped anchovy fillets, capers or chopped red pepper. I sometimes use pesto diluted with extra-virgin olive oil and lemon juice as a dressing.

1 clove garlic
Pinch of salt
6 tablespoons (90ml) extra-virgin
   olive oil
2-3 tablespoons lemon juice
Pepper to taste
1 red onion, finely chopped

1 can (14 oz. / 400g) cannellini
   or white kidney beans, drained
   and rinsed
1 can (7-oz. / 200g) tuna in oil,
   drained and coarsely flaked
Chopped parsley for garnish

1. Crush garlic with a pinch of salt, then whisk with oil, lemon juice and pepper, using a fork.
2. Mix together onion, beans and tuna, then pour the dressing over them and toss together. Sprinkle with chopped parsley.

Makes 4 servings.

Each serving contains:

Cal	Prot	Carb	Fib	Tot. Fat	Sat. Fat	Chol	Sodium
359	17g	16g	4g	25g	4g	15mg	470mg

ZUCCHINI-SHRIMP SALAD

The cool pink, red, cream and green colors correctly signal this to be an inviting light salad. It is one of the few Italian recipes that make use of mint.

Juice of 1 lemon
4 tablespoons virgin olive oil
1 tablespoon chopped parsley
Salt and pepper to taste
6 oz. (170g) small zucchini

1/2 red bell pepper
1/2 lb. (225g) peeled, cooked
  shrimp
8 mint leaves

1. Mix together lemon juice, oil, parsley, salt and pepper.
2. Cut zucchini into thin matchsticks. Cut bell pepper into thin slices and cut across the slices to halve them.
3. Toss vegetables with shrimp, mint leaves and dressing. Chill, if possible, 10 to 30 minutes.

Makes 2 servings.

Each serving contains:

Cal	Prot	Carb	Fib	Tot. Fat	Sat. Fat	Chol	Sodium
368	25g	4g	1g	28g	4g	221mg	390mg

ZUCCHINI WITH OREGANO

I like to serve crusty bread with this to mop up the cooking juices.

5 tablespoons virgin olive oil
2 cloves garlic, coarsely chopped
1-1/4 lb. (575g) small zucchini,
   thinly sliced

1/2 teaspoon dried oregano
Salt and pepper to taste
Fresh lemon juice

1. Heat oil in large skillet. Sauté garlic until lightly browned.
2. Stir zucchini into pan, then add oregano and pepper and sauté over medium-high heat, stirring frequently, about 10 minutes until zucchini are tender but still firm to the bite.
3. Add salt and lemon juice to taste. Serve with the cooking juices.

Makes 4 servings.

Each serving contains:

Cal	Prot	Carb	Fib	Tot. Fat	Sat. Fat	Chol	Sodium
175	2g	6g	2g	17g	2g	0mg	71mg

GLAZED LEEKS PARMESAN

Italians overcome the problem of watery leeks by cooking them in butter and just enough water to cover, then boiling away the water at the end of cooking so the leeks are lightly glazed. The addition of Parmesan cheese completes a beautiful dish.

*3 tablespoons (45g) unsalted
  butter, diced*
6 medium leeks, split lengthwise

*3 tablespoons freshly grated
  Parmesan cheese*
Salt and pepper to taste

1. Heat butter in a skillet or shallow flameproof casserole large enough to hold the leeks in a single layer.
2. Add leeks and water to cover. Bring to a boil, cover and cook over medium-low heat about 15 minutes, turning the leeks occasionally, until they are tender when pierced with a fork.
3. Uncover pan and boil away liquid; leeks should be slightly glazed and golden. Lightly stir in Parmesan cheese, salt and pepper.

Makes 4 servings.

Each serving contains:

Cal	Prot	Carb	Fib	Tot. Fat	Sat. Fat	Chol	Sodium
211	5g	27g	5g	11g	6g	27mg	192mg

BROCCOLI WITH CHILE AND GARLIC

Variations to this recipe include: sautéing some pine nuts until pale golden before adding the garlic and chile; cutting the garlic into fine slivers and frying it until it becomes light golden before adding the chile; adding chopped anchovy fillets, sun-dried tomatoes or finely grated Parmesan cheese just before serving.

Salt	*2-3 cloves garlic, finely chopped*
1-1/2 lb. (700g) broccoli	*1 dried red chile pepper, seeded*
3 tablespoons virgin olive oil	*and chopped*

1. Bring a large saucepan of salted water to a boil. Separate broccoli florets from stalks. Cut stalks diagonally into 1/2-inch (1.25cm) pieces and add to boiling water. Cover and boil 2 minutes. Add florets, cover and simmer 2 to 3 minutes.
2. Heat oil in a large skillet and sauté garlic and chile pepper until fragrant.
3. Drain broccoli well, tossing carefully in colander to shake off water droplets. Add to skillet and stir everything together.

Makes 4 servings.

Each serving contains:

				Tot.	Sat.		
Cal	Prot	Carb	Fib	Fat	Fat	Chol	Sodium
145	5g	11g	5g	11g	1g	0mg	114mg

FENNEL PARMESAN

In Florence, fennel used to be eaten at the end of a meal as it was believed to help digestion. It is still used this way in a few places in Tuscany, where it may be accompanied by fresh oranges or mandarins. This recipe gives a more-common way of eating fennel.

4 young fennel bulbs
3 tablespoons (45g) unsalted
  butter, diced
Juice of 1/2 lemon

Salt and pepper to taste
2 oz. (60g) freshly grated
  Parmesan cheese (1/2 cup)

1. Bring a saucepan of water to a boil.
2. Cut fennel bulbs into quarters vertically. Reserve green fronds for garnish. Add fennel quarters to saucepan and boil until tender but still slightly crisp. Drain well.
3. While fennel is cooking, preheat broiler. Put butter in shallow baking dish large enough to hold the fennel in a tightly-packed single layer, and put under broiler to melt.
4. Place fennel in dish and turn to coat with butter. Top with lemon juice, salt, pepper and cheese. Put under broiler until golden and bubbling.
5. Garnish with fennel fronds.

Makes 4 servings.

Each serving contains:

Cal	Prot	Carb	Fib	Tot. Fat	Sat. Fat	Chol	Sodium
216	9g	18g	10g	13g	8g	34mg	453mg

HERB-TOPPED TOMATOES

If you have the oven on for another dish, such as Stuffed Mushrooms, page 13, you could put this dish in when you remove the mushrooms, or a little before, then lower the oven temperature to 350F (180C) and bake about 15 minutes. The tomato pulp can be used in sauces, soups or casseroles.

2 large tomatoes
Salt
3 tablespoons fresh breadcrumbs
2 tablespoons grated Parmesan
 cheese
1 clove garlic, finely chopped

1-1/2 tablespoons chopped
 parsley
1 tablespoon chopped basil
Freshly ground black pepper
Olive oil

1. Preheat broiler.
2. Cut tomatoes in half horizontally. Scoop out pulp and set aside for another dish. Sprinkle insides of tomato shells with salt. Place upside down on paper towels to drain.
3. Combine breadcrumbs, cheese, garlic, herbs, salt and pepper to taste.
4. Place tomatoes, cut side up, in a shallow baking dish. Pile herb mixture into tomatoes and sprinkle with olive oil. Broil about 15 minutes, until tomatoes are cooked as desired.

Makes 4 servings.

Each serving contains:

Cal	Prot	Carb	Fib	Tot. Fat	Sat. Fat	Chol	Sodium
100	2g	6g	1g	8g	2g	3mg	144mg

SAUTÉED MUSHROOMS

This is a basic recipe for sautéed mushrooms, *trifolati* in Italy. It can be embellished by adding anchovy fillets for a deep, savory flavor, or wine, chopped tomatoes and/or chopped onion. Grated Parmesan cheese can be sprinkled over the mushrooms before serving. Basil, thyme or rosemary can be substituted for the parsley.

4 tablespoons virgin olive oil
1-1/2 to 2 cloves garlic, finely
chopped
1-1/2 lb. (700g) fresh mushrooms,
sliced

3 tablespoons finely chopped
parsley
Salt and pepper to taste

1. Heat oil in a skillet large enough to hold mushrooms without crowding them. Add garlic and cook until lightly colored but not brown.
2. Add mushrooms and fry, shaking pan and stirring mushrooms frequently, about 5 minutes; do not overcook.
3. Stir in parsley, salt and pepper.

Makes 4 servings.

Each serving contains:

Cal	Prot	Carb	Fib	Tot. Fat	Sat. Fat	Chol	Sodium
164	4g	8g	2g	14g	2g	0mg	74mg

SAVORY FLORENTINE MUSHROOMS

The mushrooms should have a subtle deep, savory, almost meaty flavor, which can be achieved by cooking them slowly for a long time. This recipe produces the same result quickly by following the simple old custom of adding anchovies to dishes to enhance their flavor.

3 tablespoons virgin olive oil
1/2 red onion or 1 shallot, finely chopped
1 clove garlic, minced
1 lb. (450g) fresh mushrooms, sliced

2 tomatoes
5 anchovy fillets, chopped
1-1/2 tablespoons chopped parsley
Freshly ground black pepper

1. Heat oil in a large skillet. Add onion or shallot and cook until softened.
2. Add garlic and cook 1 minute until fragrant. Add mushrooms and cook, stirring occasionally, until juices have evaporated.
3. Seed and chop tomatoes, peeling them first if preferred.
4. Push mushrooms to one side of skillet. Add anchovies to bare area and mash with a wooden spoon. Add tomatoes and most of the parsley and mix well. Simmer gently about 5 minutes.
5. Season generously with black pepper; salt will probably not be necessary because of the saltiness of the anchovies. Serve sprinkled with remaining parsley.

Makes 4 servings.

Each serving contains:

Cal	Prot	Carb	Fib	Tot. Fat	Sat. Fat	Chol	Sodium
148	5g	10g	2g	11g	2g	4mg	194mg

SPINACH PARMESAN

This dish is one of the most quintessentially Italian. It can really only be made with fresh spinach leaves. Fortunately, this is now possible for most of the year.

2 lb. (900g) small spinach leaves
1/4 cup (60g) unsalted butter
Salt and pepper to taste

Freshly grated nutmeg
1-1/2 oz. (45g) grated Parmesan
*   cheese (6 tablespoons)*

1. Wash spinach and shake off excess moisture.
2. Melt butter in a saucepan, add spinach with just the water clinging to the leaves and cook, stirring occasionally, 2 to 3 minutes, until spinach is tender.
3. Season with a little salt, plenty of pepper and a pinch of nutmeg. Sprinkle with Parmesan and serve.

Makes 4 servings.

Each serving contains:

Cal	Prot	Carb	Fib	Tot. Fat	Sat. Fat	Chol	Sodium
200	11g	8g	6g	15g	9g	39mg	445mg

SICILIAN SPINACH

The use of pine nuts and raisins pinpoints this as being a typically Sicilian dish.

2 lb. (900g) small spinach leaves
3 tablespoons virgin olive oil
1 clove garlic, crushed
4 tablespoons pine nuts

3 tablespoons raisins
Salt and pepper to taste
Juice of 1/2 lemon (optional)

1. Wash spinach and shake off excess moisture. Put spinach into large saucepan with just the water clinging to the leaves and cook over medium heat, stirring occasionally, until wilted. Drain well.
2. Heat oil in skillet, add garlic and sauté until golden. Remove garlic and discard. Add pine nuts.
3. When nuts are brown, stir in raisins, then add spinach, salt, pepper and lemon juice, if using. Stir together and serve.

Makes 4 servings.

Each serving contains:

Cal	Prot	Carb	Fib	Tot. Fat	Sat. Fat	Chol	Sodium
234	10g	16g	7g	18g	3g	0mg	247mg

CAULIFLOWER WITH OLIVES AND ANCHOVIES

This simple treatment turns cauliflower into a piquant, savory accompaniment for lamb or pork.

1 lb. (450g) cauliflower florets
3/4 can (2-oz. / 60g) anchovy
  fillets
1 small onion, minced
1 clove garlic

5-6 pitted black olives
1 tablespoon capers, drained
1-1/2 tablespoons chopped
  parsley
Freshly ground black pepper

1. Bring a large saucepan of water to a boil.
2. Place cauliflower in saucepan, cover and return quickly to a boil. Boil 5 to 7 minutes until just tender.
3. Drain oil from anchovies into a small skillet and heat. Add onion and sauté until softened.
4. Crush garlic and anchovies to make a paste. Stir into skillet and add olives, capers, parsley and pepper. Heat gently.
5. Drain cauliflower and place in warm serving dish. Pour anchovy mixture over cauliflower and toss lightly.

Makes 4 servings.

Each serving contains:

Cal	Prot	Carb	Fib	Tot. Fat	Sat. Fat	Chol	Sodium
64	5g	7g	2g	3g	1g	9mg	545mg

BRAISED RADICCHIO WITH PANCETTA

Cooking radicchio gives it a richer flavor. However, this gain is at the expense of its beautiful, characteristic burgundy color and distinctive white markings as it becomes tawny red. Serve the radicchio with good bread to mop up the juices.

2 tablespoons virgin olive oil
2 oz. (60g) pancetta or thick-cut
   bacon, diced
1/2 small onion, minced
1 clove garlic, minced

2 heads radicchio
2 tablespoons red-wine vinegar
1 tablespoon balsamic vinegar
1 teaspoon sugar
Salt and pepper to taste

1. Heat oil in large skillet. Add pancetta or bacon and cook 1 to 2 minutes. Add onion and garlic and cook until bacon is browned at the edges and onion is soft.
2. Divide each radicchio head into 8 wedges, cut through the core.
3. Stir vinegars, sugar and 3 tablespoons water into skillet, then add radicchio, packing it in a single layer. Bring to a boil, cover and cook about 12 minutes, turning radicchio halfway through.
4. Remove lid and cook gently until liquid is reduced as desired. Season with salt and pepper and serve warm.

Makes 4 servings.

Each serving contains:

Cal	Prot	Carb	Fib	Tot. Fat	Sat. Fat	Chol	Sodium
151	5g	14g	0g	10g	2g	4mg	192mg

SAUTÉED RED PEPPERS

Sautéing red peppers brings out their sweetness, which is further enhanced by a judicious splash of sweet-sharp balsamic vinegar. This makes a good accompaniment to Lamb Cutlets with Herbs, page 106, or Mullet with Parma Ham, page 83.

3 tablespoons olive oil	*1-1/2 teaspoons balsamic vinegar*
1 large red onion, thinly sliced	*Chopped basil or parsley*
2 red bell peppers, thinly sliced	*Salt and pepper to taste*
1 clove garlic, chopped	

1. Heat oil in large skillet and sauté onion until softened but not colored.
2. Add peppers and sauté briskly until tender and browned in patches. Add garlic about halfway through the cooking.
3. Pour contents of the pan into a warm serving dish and sprinkle with balsamic vinegar, basil or parsley, salt and pepper.

Makes 4 servings.

Each serving contains:

Cal	Prot	Carb	Fib	Tot. Fat	Sat. Fat	Chol	Sodium
112	1g	5g	1g	10g	1g	0mg	68mg

CELERY WITH PANCETTA AND TOMATOES

For even cooking, choose celery stalks that are all the same size—I prefer to use medium-size ones. However, if you are using heads of celery and therefore have celery stalks of different sizes, start cooking the fatter stalks before adding the thinner ones.

4 tablespoons olive oil
2 onions, thinly sliced
2 oz. (60g) pancetta or unsmoked
* bacon, cut into strips*
2 tomatoes, chopped
1-2 sun-dried tomato halves,
* sliced (optional)*

1 lb. (450g) celery stalks, cut into
* 3-inch (7.5cm) lengths*
Salt and pepper to taste
Black olives, preferably oil-cured,
* or chopped parsley for garnish*

1. Heat oil in a flameproof shallow casserole or deep skillet and sauté onions until softened and lightly colored.
2. Add pancetta or bacon and cook briskly until fat becomes translucent.
3. Stir in tomatoes, including seeds and juice, sun-dried tomatoes, if using, celery, salt and pepper. Cover and cook over moderate heat about 20 minutes, shaking the pan occasionally, until celery is tender. Remove lid, increase heat and stir to reduce liquid to desired consistency.
4. Serve garnished with black olives or chopped parsley.

Makes 4 servings.

Each serving contains:

Cal	Prot	Carb	Fib	Tot. Fat	Sat. Fat	Chol	Sodium
198	4g	12g	4g	16g	2g	5mg	389mg

BROCCOLI PARMESAN

The Italians are credited with bringing broccoli seeds to North America. Over the years this versatile vegetable has gained tremendous popularity.

1-1/2 lb. (700g) fresh broccoli or
  2 pkg. (10-oz. / 280g) frozen
  broccoli spears
3 tablespoons olive oil
3 tablespoons butter

1 garlic clove, minced
2 tablespoons pine nuts
3 tablespoons wine vinegar
Grated Parmesan cheese
Salt and pepper to taste

1. Peel off tough outer skin of fresh broccoli stems. Break off florets ands cut stems into 2-inch (5cm) pieces.
2. Steam fresh broccoli 8 to 10 minutes. Cook frozen broccoli as directed on package.
3. In a skillet, heat oil and butter; sauté garlic and pine nuts. Remove from heat and stir in vinegar.
4. Place broccoli in serving bowl. Add oil mixture and toss. Sprinkle with Parmesan cheese and season with salt and pepper.

Makes 4 servings.

Each serving contains:

Cal	Prot	Carb	Fib	Tot. Fat	Sat. Fat	Chol	Sodium
283	10g	11g	5g	25g	9g	28mg	317mg

Chapter Three

PASTA AND PIZZA

The conventional use for pasta is as a first course, but today's less-structured meals and more-casual lifestyles, coupled with a widening range of pasta recipes, mean that pasta dishes now are also served as snacks, main courses or side dishes.

Pizzas make marvelous snacks or main courses. Prepackaged, ready-made crusts may not be as good as homemade ones. But if you add plenty of good, tasty topping ingredients, they provide the starting point for quickly prepared and interesting dishes with the expenditure of very little effort or time.

To help ensure that cooked pasta has a good texture and to prevent it sticking, allow 1 quart (1 liter) water to each 4 ounces (115g) pasta. Bring the water to a rolling boil. Add the pasta all at once, give it a stir with a fork to separate it, then cover the pan and quickly bring the water to a boil again. After that, uncover the pan and cook the pasta until it is just tender but still firm to the bite. The time that this takes will depend on whether the pasta is fresh or dried, its thickness and shape, and the brand.

SPAGHETTI WITH GARLIC CRUMBS *good - use*
lots more garlic + herbs

A simple but surprisingly effective pasta dish. The number of people it serves depends on whether it is to be eaten as a snack or light meal or as an accompaniment to another dish such as Steak Pizzaiola, page 109.

more

2-3 tablespoons virgin olive oil
2 cloves garlic, crushed
1-1/2 cups (85g) fresh
*   breadcrumbs*
3/4 lb. (340g) spaghetti

Chopped herbs, such as parsley,
*   tarragon, basil or chervil*
Coarsely ground black pepper
Freshly grated Parmesan cheese

1. Heat 2 tablespoons oil in a skillet, add garlic and breadcrumbs and sauté, stirring frequently, until crumbs are crisp and brown; add a little more oil if necessary and be careful not to burn garlic and breadcrumbs.
2. Cook spaghetti according to package directions.
3. Drain spaghetti and toss with herbs and pepper. Scatter breadcrumbs over spaghetti, toss briefly and serve with freshly grated Parmesan.

Makes 4 servings as a side dish.

Each serving contains:

Cal	Prot	Carb	Fib	Tot. Fat	Sat. Fat	Chol	Sodium
286	8g	33g	1g	13g	3g	5mg	269mg

HERB CARBONARA

The residual heat in the pasta and pan should be sufficient to cook the egg so it gives a thick, creamy coating to the tagliatelle. You can put the pan over a very low heat, but be careful not to overcook the eggs.

10-12 oz. (280-340g) tagliatelle
6 tablespoons (90ml) extra-virgin olive oil
3 oz. (85g) grated pecorino or Parmesan cheese (3/4 cup)
4 egg yolks

2 cloves garlic, crushed
2 tablespoons chopped chives
2 tablespoons chopped basil
2 tablespoons chopped marjoram
Freshly ground black pepper

1. Cook tagliatelle according to package directions.
2. Combine remaining ingredients.
3. Drain tagliatelle and return to pan. Immediately add cheese mixture and toss it through the pasta using 2 forks. If desired, put pan over very low heat for a minute or two, shaking and tossing pan until eggs are cooked.

Makes 3 to 4 servings.

Each serving contains:

Cal	Prot	Carb	Fib	Tot. Fat	Sat. Fat	Chol	Sodium
607	21g	33g	2g	43g	11g	306mg	538mg

PASTA WITH BROCCOLI AND HAM

This recipe uses the same method as Herb Carbonara, page 57, so it is important to work quickly after the ingredients have been brought together, or to reheat them very gently. The sauce that bathes the pasta and broccoli is made extra-creamy by the addition of soft cheese.

1/2 lb. (225g) pasta shells	*Salt and pepper to taste*
1/2 lb. (225g) broccoli florets	*1 oz. (30g) cream cheese or*
2 oz. (60g) Parma ham, chopped	*goat cheese*
3 eggs, at room temperature	*Freshly grated Parmesan cheese*

1. Cook tagliatelle according to package directions until tender but still firm to the bite. Cook broccoli in medium-size saucepan, timing it to be ready at the same time as the pasta.
2. Beat ham, eggs and pepper together.
3. Quickly drain broccoli and pasta and put into pan in which pasta was cooked. Immediately stir in egg-and-ham mixture and soft cheese. If sauce does not begin to thicken, put pan over very low heat and shake and toss until sauce shows signs of thickening. Serve immediately with freshly grated Parmesan cheese.

Makes 2 to 3 servings.

Each serving contains:

				Tot.	Sat.		
Cal	Prot	Carb	Fib	Fat	Fat	Chol	Sodium
414	26g	40g	5g	17g	7g	350mg	551mg

PASTA WITH BROCCOLI AND GORGONZOLA

Instead of milk, try using 1/4 cup (60ml) half-and-half or whipping cream or 3/4 cup (185ml) dry white wine boiled until reduced by half.

Salt
3/4 lb. (340g) broccoli
12 oz. (340g) pasta shells
6 oz. (170g) Gorgonzola cheese, chopped

1/4 cup (60ml) milk
1 tablespoon (15g) unsalted butter
Pepper to taste
1/3 cup (40g) chopped walnuts

1. Bring 2 large saucepans of salted water to a boil.
2. Divide broccoli into florets. Trim stalks and slice thinly on the diagonal. Add to one of the pans, cover and return quickly to a boil. Boil until tender.
3. Add pasta to second pan of water, stir, cover pan and return to boil. Remove lid and cook according to package instructions until tender but still firm to the bite. Time it to be ready at the same time as the broccoli.
4. While broccoli and pasta are cooking, heat cheese gently with milk and butter, stirring until smooth; do not allow to boil. Season with pepper.
5. Drain broccoli and pasta, then toss together with cheese sauce and walnuts.

Makes 4 servings.

Each serving contains:

Cal	Prot	Carb	Fib	Tot. Fat	Sat. Fat	Chol	Sodium
396	19g	31g	4g	23g	11g	46mg	801mg

FUSILLI WITH ZUCCHINI AND MOZZARELLA

Although the ingredients are available throughout the year, I always feel this is a *summer* pasta dish—not only because it is light and fresh tasting but because zucchini, tomatoes and herbs are at their best then.

12 oz. (340g) fusilli	5 oz. (145g) mozzarella cheese,
Salt	chopped
2 medium zucchini, thinly sliced	2 teaspoons chopped parsley
4 tablespoons virgin olive oil	1 tablespoon chopped basil
2 small cloves garlic, crushed	Juice of 1/2 lemon
2 tomatoes, chopped	Pepper to taste

1. Add fusilli to a pan of salted, boiling water, stir, cover pan and return to boil. Remove lid and cook 4 to 5 minutes if fresh, 8 to 9 minutes if dried, until tender but still firm to the bite.
2. Sauté zucchini in 2 tablespoons oil 2 to 3 minutes.
3. Add garlic and tomatoes and cook 2 minutes, until zucchini is tender and tomatoes are heated.
4. Drain the fusilli and toss with cheese, herbs, lemon juice, zucchini, tomatoes and remaining oil. Season with salt and pepper and serve.

Makes 4 servings.

Each serving contains:

Cal	Prot	Carb	Fib	Tot. Fat	Sat. Fat	Chol	Sodium
366	13g	31g	3g	22g	7g	28mg	208mg

SPAGHETTI WITH PANCETTA AND WALNUTS

This is quite a substantial pasta dish so it is suitable for a light meal, possibly followed by a simple salad, or it could be served as a main course. You can use soft, medium or firm goat cheese, or goat cheese that has been kept in oil, depending on your preference.

Salt
3 tablespoons olive oil
1/2 lb. (225g) pancetta or smoked
  bacon, chopped
1 clove garlic, crushed
3/4 cup (85g) walnuts, coarsely
  chopped
1/2 onion, chopped

12 oz. (340g) spaghetti
1 lb. (450g) tomatoes, seeded
  and chopped
Grated zest of 1 lemon
4 tablespoons chopped parsley
Freshly ground black pepper
8 oz. (225g) soft goat cheese,
  chopped

1. Bring a large saucepan of salted water to a boil.
2. Heat oil in a skillet, add pancetta or bacon and start to fry it.
3. Add garlic, walnuts and onion and sauté until golden.
4. Add spaghetti to boiling water, stir, cover and return to boil. Remove lid and cook 3 to 4 minutes if fresh, about 8 minutes if dried, until tender but still firm to the bite.
5. Add tomatoes, lemon zest, parsley and pepper to skillet and heat gently 2 to 3 minutes to warm through.
6. Drain spaghetti and toss with tomato mixture and cheese. Serve immediately.

Makes 4 servings.

Each serving contains:

Cal	Prot	Carb	Fib	Tot. Fat	Sat. Fat	Chol	Sodium
636	24g	35g	3g	45g	14g	42mg	521mg

PASTA WITH SCALLOPS AND PESTO

This recipe fits the bill when I want something impressive, but have only a short time in which to prepare and cook it. An additional advantage is that it uses ingredients you probably have on hand.

Salt
2 cloves garlic
1 shallot or 1/2 small onion,
  coarsely chopped
1-1/2 cups (45g) basil leaves
4 sun-dried tomato halves,
  packed in oil
2 tablespoons oil from the tomatoes
7 tablespoons (100ml) extra-
  virgin olive oil

1/4 cup (30g) walnut halves
2 tablespoons pine nuts or
  almond halves
5 tablespoons freshly grated
  Parmesan cheese
Pepper to taste
1 lb. (450g) shelled small scallops
14 oz. (400g) pappardelle or
  other ribbon noodles

1. Bring a large saucepan of salted water to a boil.
2. To make pesto: With motor running, drop garlic into blender and process until coarsely chopped. Add shallot or onion, basil, sun-dried tomatoes, sun-dried-tomato oil, 5 tablespoons olive oil and nuts. Mix until fairly smooth. Scoop into a bowl and stir in cheese and plenty of pepper but only a little salt.
3. Chop 4 ounces (115g) of the scallops. Heat remaining oil in a large nonstick skillet. Place whole scallops in skillet and fry, stirring frequently, 2 minutes. Add chopped scallops and cook 1 to 2 minutes, until just translucent. Remove pan from heat.
4. While scallops are cooking, add pasta to boiling water, stir, cover the pan and return to a boil. Remove lid and cook according to package instructions until tender but still firm to the bite.
5. Drain pasta and toss with scallops and pesto.

Makes 4 servings.

Each serving contains:

				Tot.	Sat.		
Cal	Prot	Carb	Fib	Fat	Fat	Chol	Sodium
593	21g	34g	3g	43g	7g	24mg	455mg

PASTA WITH TUNA

Make the sauce more intense by using the red pepper and mashing 4 chopped anchovy fillets into the pan with it so they dissolve. Use 3 tomatoes if you include the red pepper, 4 tomatoes if you leave it out. For a treat, you could use 1 pound (450g) diced fresh tuna; fry it until lightly browned and just cooked through.

Salt to taste
2 tablespoons virgin olive oil
1 clove garlic, cut into fine slivers
1 red pepper, broiled, peeled,
  chopped or sliced (optional)
1 can (7-oz. / 200g) tuna, drained
3 or 4 tomatoes, depending on
  whether red pepper is used

10-12 black olives, preferably
  oil-cured, pits removed
10 oz. (280g) penne or other
  short tubes, or pasta shapes
Leaves from a large sprig of basil,
  chopped
Pepper to taste

1. Bring a large saucepan of salted water to a boil.
2. Heat oil in a skillet and add garlic and red pepper, if using. If pepper has not been broiled, cook it until it begins to soften.
3. Flake tuna, seed and chop tomatoes and slice olives lengthwise. Add pasta to boiling water, stir, cover pan and return to boil. Remove lid and cook according to package instructions until tender but still firm to the bite.
4. Add tomatoes, tuna, olives, basil, salt and pepper to skillet and cook gently about 2 minutes.
5. Drain pasta and return to pan. Toss in sauce and serve.

Makes 4 servings.

Each serving contains:

Cal	Prot	Carb	Fib	Tot. Fat	Sat. Fat	Chol	Sodium
294	18g	27g	3g	13g	2g	15mg	393mg

PASTA WITH SMOKED TROUT AND PEPPERS

Broiled peppers have an intriguing sweet-smoky taste that complements the more-pronounced taste of smoked trout.

2-1/2 large red bell peppers
Salt
14 oz. (400g) fettucine or other
* ribbon pasta*
4 tablespoons virgin olive oil

4 tablespoons pine nuts
6-8 oz. (170-225g) smoked trout
* fillets, flaked*
2 tablespoons chopped basil
Freshly ground black pepper

1. Preheat broiler. Halve red peppers and broil until charred and blistered. Let cool slightly, then remove the skin, holding peppers over a bowl to catch juice. Thinly slice peppers.
2. Bring a large saucepan of salted water to a boil. Add pasta, stir, cover pan and return to boil. Remove lid and cook according to package instructions until tender but still firm to the bite.
3. While pasta is cooking, heat oil in a large saucepan.
4. Add pepper strips and reserved juice and pine nuts to oil. Heat gently 1 minute, then add trout. Cover and remove from heat.
5. Drain pasta and add to peppers and trout. Add basil and black pepper. Toss to mix, and serve.

Makes 4 servings.

Each serving contains:

Cal	Prot	Carb	Fib	Tot. Fat	Sat. Fat	Chol	Sodium
428	20g	33g	3g	25g	4g	32mg	32mg

PASTA WITH SAUSAGES

This is a favorite recipe for when I have walked the dog longer than I intended, or when I am in the middle of a hard day's gardening and want something quick, tasty and sustaining.

2 tablespoons olive oil
1 onion, sliced
2 cloves garlic, crushed
Salt to taste
3/4 to 1 lb. (340-450g) fresh hot
  Italian sausages

8 oz. (250ml) tomato sauce
12 oz. (340g) pasta shells
2-3 tablespoons chopped parsley
Pepper to taste
Freshly grated Parmesan cheese

1. Heat oil in skillet and sauté onion and garlic until soft.
2. Bring a large saucepan of salted water to a boil.
3. Remove skin from sausages; chop sausage meat into large pieces. Add to onion and cook over high heat, stirring, until browned.
4. Stir in tomato sauce, bring to a boil, cover and simmer about 15 minutes.
5. Add pasta to boiling water, stir, cover pan and return to boil. Remove lid and cook according to package instructions until tender but still firm to the bite.
6. Stir parsley, salt and pepper into sauce.
7. Drain pasta and pour into a warm serving bowl. Pour sauce over pasta and toss lightly. Serve with grated Parmesan cheese.

Makes 4 servings.

Variation

Pasta with Salami—Omit fresh sausages and use 6 oz. (170g) chopped salami instead. If desired, sauté a chopped red chile pepper with the onion and garlic, or add a dash of chili sauce with the tomato sauce.

Each serving contains:

Cal	Prot	Carb	Fib	Tot. Fat	Sat. Fat	Chol	Sodium
463	21g	40g	4g	25g	8g	50mg	1236mg

DOUBLE-MUSHROOM AND SAUSAGE PASTA

Fresh and dried mushrooms are brought together in an uncomplicated sauce. If you like, use hot wine as the soaking liquid for the dried mushrooms.

3-4 dried porcini mushrooms
1 cup (250ml) hot water
1 lb. (450g) sweet Italian sausage
1 leek, sliced (white part only),
   or 1/2 onion, chopped
1 can (16-oz. / 450g) tomatoes

1 tablespoon basil or oregano
1/2 lb. (225g) fresh mushrooms,
   chopped
2 tablespoons capers, drained
Salt and pepper to taste
12 oz. (340g) pasta, cooked

1. Soak dried mushrooms in hot water.
2. Remove casing from sausage. Brown sausage meat in a skillet, breaking up large pieces.
3. Add leek or onion and sauté. Stir in tomatoes, with juice, and basil or oregano.
4. Chop soaked mushrooms and add, with liquid, to skillet. Cook about 15 minutes, until mushrooms are tender.
5. Add remaining ingredients and cook 5 to 8 minutes longer.
6. Spoon sauce over cooked pasta.

Makes 4 servings.

Each serving contains:

Cal	Prot	Carb	Fib	Tot. Fat	Sat. Fat	Chol	Sodium
605	27g	40g	5g	37g	13g	86mg	1249mg

PIZZA WITH TOMATOES AND GARLIC

This is a pizza to eat with a knife and fork, not in your fingers, as you will need to mash the garlic cloves while you eat the pizza. Instead of using a ready-made pizza crust, you could use a mix (or, when you have plenty of time, make your own crust) and work in 1-1/2 tablespoons chopped mixed herbs.

4 tomatoes, chopped
1 teaspoon salt
1 bulb of garlic
1-1/2 to 2 tablespoons virgin
   olive oil
1 pizza crust, frozen, made from
   mix or homemade
Flour

8 black olives, preferably
   oil-cured
Leaves from a small sprig of
   rosemary, chopped
3 oz. (85g) mozzarella cheese,
   chopped
Pepper to taste
Fresh basil leaves

1. Preheat oven according to pizza-crust instructions.
2. Combine tomatoes and salt in a bowl; set aside.
3. Divide garlic into cloves and mix with oil.
4. Roll crust out to a circle 10 inches (25cm) in diameter. Place on a lightly floured baking sheet or pizza pan.
5. Spoon tomatoes onto crust and scatter the garlic cloves, olives, rosemary and cheese over them.
6. Bake about 20 minutes or according to package instructions.
7. Season with plenty of pepper and garnish with basil leaves.

Makes 2 servings.

Each serving contains:

Cal	Prot	Carb	Fib	Tot. Fat	Sat. Fat	Chol	Sodium
375	12g	23g	4g	28g	9g	34mg	514mg

EGGPLANT-SALAMI PIZZA

Instead of using chopped herbs to flavor the tomato sauce, you could use 4 to 5 tablespoons pesto. Or substitute 6 tablespoons drained canned chopped tomatoes with herbs for the tomato sauce.

*2 ready-made pizza crusts, each
  8 inches (20cm) in diameter
6 tablespoons tomato sauce
2 teaspoons chopped parsley,
  basil or thyme
Salt and pepper to taste
1 small eggplant, about 6 oz.
  (170g), thinly sliced*

*5 oz. (145g) salami, thinly sliced
5 oz. (145g) goat cheese,
  crumbled
8 black olives, preferably
  oil-cured
8 basil leaves, coarsely shredded*

1. Preheat oven according to pizza-crust instructions. Place crusts on pizza pans or large baking sheet.
2. Mix tomato sauce with herbs, salt and pepper; spread over pizza crusts. Cover with alternating slices of eggplant and salami. Top with goat cheese, olives and pepper.
3. Bake about 20 minutes or according to instructions on package. Sprinkle with basil a few minutes before end of cooking time.

Makes 2 to 4 servings.

Each serving contains:

Cal	Prot	Carb	Fib	Tot. Fat	Sat. Fat	Chol	Sodium
315	17g	10g	1g	23g	12g	61mg	865mg

Chapter Four

FISH

Fish is an ideal food for cooking quickly and also fits the trend toward a light, healthful diet. Portions and fillets cook more quickly than whole fish, but their quality deteriorates quickly, so always try to buy ones that have been prepared especially for you. Italy's long coastline means that fish and shellfish feature prominently in Italian diets, especially near the coast. Inland, from central Italy northward, streams that tumble down from the mountains provide freshwater fish such as trout.

Unfortunately, many varieties of fish, and particularly shellfish and crustaceans, from the Adriatic and Mediterranean seas are difficult—and expensive—to find outside Italy and southern Europe. So for some recipes I have used more-readily available ones that lend themselves to Italian recipes.

SEA BASS WITH LEMON AND MARJORAM

Several varieties of fish are found around the Italian coast. Sea bass are ideally suited to this light, simple recipe, but you could use small sea bream or petrale sole or, in a pinch, trout.

1/4 cup (60g) unsalted butter, diced
4 sea bass, each about 12 oz. (340g)
3 cloves garlic, lightly crushed

1 teaspoon chopped marjoram
1 tablespoon lemon juice
Salt and pepper to taste
Lemon wedges

1. Melt butter in a skillet large enough to hold the fish in a single layer. Add fish, garlic and marjoram and cook for 4 minutes, turning the fish halfway through.
2. Add lemon juice and pepper, cover pan and cook 10 to 12 minutes, again turning fish halfway through.
3. Season fish with salt and pepper and transfer to a warm serving plate. Top with cooking juices and serve with lemon wedges.

Makes 4 servings.

Each serving contains:

Cal	Prot	Carb	Fib	Tot. Fat	Sat. Fat	Chol	Sodium
389	54g	1g	0g	17g	9g	152mg	268mg

FISH WITH ZUCCHINI

Hake is the common Mediterranean white fish. It has a fairly soft, white flesh and delicate flavor. If you are unable to find it or would prefer cod or halibut, either of these can be used instead.

2 hake, cod or halibut steaks,
each 5-6 oz. (145-170g)
Salt and pepper to taste
2 tablespoons olive oil, plus extra
for brushing
1/2 small red onion, minced
1 clove garlic, chopped

1/2 cup (125ml) fish stock
1/2 cup (125ml) dry white wine
9 oz. (250g) small zucchini
1 tomato, seeded and chopped
3 anchovy fillets, chopped
1/2 tablespoon chopped basil
1/2 tablespoon chopped parsley

1. Preheat broiler or grill. Season fish with salt and pepper and brush lightly with oil. Broil or grill about 5 minutes on each side, until flesh flakes when tested with a fork.
2. Heat oil in a skillet or wide saucepan. Sauté onion and garlic until soft but not colored. Add stock and wine and boil until reduced to about one-third (6 tablespoons). Add zucchini and cook until tender-crisp.
3. Add tomato, anchovies, herbs and more salt and pepper to cooked zucchini. Heat about 1 minute.
4. Transfer mixture to two warmed plates and put fish on top.

Makes 2 servings.

Each serving contains:

Cal	Prot	Carb	Fib	Tot. Fat	Sat. Fat	Chol	Sodium
427	23g	12g	3g	29g	4g	50mg	433mg

FRIED COD WITH WARM SALSA

The flavored sauce goes well with the firm, large flakes of cod, making a dish that tastes satisfying yet is neither rich nor heavy.

1 tablespoon olive oil
4 cod cutlets or steaks, each
   5-6 oz. (145-170g)
2 anchovy fillets, minced
3 cloves garlic, crushed
1 tablespoon chopped basil
2 tablespoons chopped parsley

1-1/2 tablespoons capers, drained
1-1/4 teaspoons English mustard
4 tablespoons lemon juice
2 tablespoons virgin or
   extra-virgin olive oil
Pepper to taste

1. Heat olive oil in a nonstick skillet. Add cod and cook about 5 minutes on each side, until flesh flakes easily when tested with a fork.
2. Crush anchovy fillets with garlic and basil to make a paste. Mix in parsley, capers, mustard, lemon juice, oil and pepper.
3. Pour sauce around fish and warm through briefly.
4. Remove fish from skillet and serve with sauce poured over.

Makes 4 servings.

Each serving contains:

Cal	Prot	Carb	Fib	Tot. Fat	Sat. Fat	Chol	Sodium
237	31g	1g	0g	11g	2g	75mg	284mg

FISH WITH EGG-AND-BASIL SAUCE

Save time by making the sauce and cooking the eggs in advance. But don't leave the eggs to cool in the cooking water because this may cause unsightly gray-black rings around the yolks.

2 large eggs, room temperature
8 lemon sole or flounder fillets,
  each about 5 oz. (145g)
Salt and pepper to taste
Virgin olive oil

1/2 cup (15g) minced basil
1 clove garlic, minced
3 oz. (85g) grated Parmesan
  cheese (3/4 cup)

1. Bring a small saucepan of water to a boil, then add eggs and simmer 8 to 10 minutes, depending on whether you want the yolks slightly creamy or hard.
2. Preheat broiler or grill. Season fish with salt and pepper and lightly flatten with a spatula. Fold each one in half, brush with oil and broil or grill 8 to 10 minutes, turning fish halfway through.
3. Drain eggs and rinse under running cold water until cool enough to peel. Peel and chop eggs, then mix with basil, garlic and cheese. Beat in enough oil to make a soft sauce that will hold its shape. Season with plenty of pepper.
4. Serve sauce with fish.

Makes 4 servings.

Each serving contains:

Cal	Prot	Carb	Fib	Tot. Fat	Sat. Fat	Chol	Sodium
483	65g	1g	0g	22g	7g	259mg	724mg

FISH WITH POLENTA CRUST

Coarse polenta makes a delicious, crisp coating that keeps the fish succulent during cooking. To vary the sauce add some sun-dried-tomato paste or a dash of balsamic vinegar.

Coarse polenta
Salt and pepper to taste
4 skinned fish fillets, each
   5-6 oz. (145-170g)
1 egg, beaten
Olive oil and unsalted butter for
   frying

BASIL-OLIVE VINAIGRETTE
1 clove garlic

1/2 cup (125ml) extra-virgin
   olive oil
1-1/2 tablespoons red-wine
   vinegar
1 tablespoon chopped basil or
   parsley
1/2 lb. (225g) tomatoes, seeded
   and finely chopped
10-12 pitted black olives,
   preferably oil-cured, chopped

1. Make vinaigrette: Crush garlic with a pinch of salt; add oil, vinegar, basil or parsley, tomatoes, olives and pepper to taste.
2. Season polenta with salt and pepper; put a thick layer on a plate.
3. Season fish with salt and pepper, dip in beaten egg and allow excess to drain off. Press both sides of fish into polenta to coat lightly, evenly and firmly.
4. Heat a shallow layer of oil and butter in a skillet. Add fish and cook about 3 minutes on each side.
5. Serve fish with vinaigrette.

Makes 4 servings.

Each serving contains:

Cal	Prot	Carb	Fib	Tot. Fat	Sat. Fat	Chol	Sodium
590	34g	15g	2g	44g	9g	142mg	402mg

SCALLOPS WITH CAPER VINAIGRETTE

The piquant vinaigrette is made while the scallops are cooking, so the dish is very quickly prepared. This is also a good way to cook fish such as salmon, flounder and sole.

1 tablespoon (15g) butter
2 tablespoons olive oil
1 lb. (450g) scallops
Salt and pepper to taste
1 tomato, seeded and chopped
1 heaping teaspoon capers, coarsely chopped

1/2 small red onion or 1 small shallot or 1/4 onion, chopped
1-1/2 teaspoons chopped parsley
1 teaspoon chopped basil
2 tablespoons white-wine vinegar
4 tablespoons virgin olive oil

1. Heat butter and oil in a wide skillet. Season scallops with salt and pepper, add to pan and cook until lightly browned.
2. Combine remaining ingredients.
3. Transfer scallops to warm plates and serve with sauce poured over them.

Makes 2 servings.

Each serving contains:

Cal	Prot	Carb	Fib	Tot. Fat	Sat. Fat	Chol	Sodium
558	19g	9g	1g	50g	10g	52mg	716mg

MACKEREL WITH OLIVES AND TOMATOES

The tomatoes are not cooked down to a sauce. They are heated briefly with the olives, garlic and herbs so that they are warm but still retain their shape. The heat brings out the flavor of the ingredients to make a kind of warm, fragrant relish.

1 tablespoon olive oil
4 mackerel fillets, each about
  4 oz. (115g)
Salt and pepper to taste
2 tablespoons (30g) unsalted butter
1 clove garlic, crushed

4 tomatoes, seeded and chopped
8 pitted black olives, sliced
Juice of 1/2 lemon
1 tablespoon chopped parsley
1 teaspoon chopped thyme leaves

1. Heat oil in a nonstick skillet. With point of a sharp knife, cut 2 or 3 slashes in skin of each fillet. Place in pan, skin side down, and fry until golden. Turn fillets over and fry on other side. Using a spatula, transfer fish to a warm plate, season with salt and pepper and keep warm.
3. Add butter to skillet. When it is foaming, add garlic, tomatoes and olives. Heat 1 to 2 minutes, shaking the pan. Add lemon juice, herbs and more salt and pepper. Pour over fish and serve.

Makes 4 servings.

Each serving contains:

Cal	Prot	Carb	Fib	Tot. Fat	Sat. Fat	Chol	Sodium
350	22g	7g	2g	26g	8g	95mg	259mg

TROTA DEL NERA

The River Nera in Umbria, one of seven land-locked Italian provinces, was traditionally the source of wild trout. They had such a fine flavor and succulent flesh that they were cooked and served quite plainly to highlight their quality. Today farmed trout are widely available. These less-distinguished fish need more help if they are to make memorable dishes—this modern recipe adds a vibrant salad.

4 trout, each about 10 oz. (280g)
3/4 cup (185ml) virgin olive oil,
  plus extra for brushing
1 lemon, halved
1/2 red onion, coarsely chopped
1 clove garlic
10 capers

16 oil-cured black olives, pitted
4 sun-dried tomato halves
1 tablespoon red-wine vinegar
Leaves from a very large bunch of
  Italian parsley
Salt and pepper to taste
Lemon wedges

1. Preheat broiler or grill. With point of sharp knife, cut 3 slashes in both sides of each trout. Brush trout with olive oil, squeeze lemon juice over them and broil or grill 5 to 7 minutes on each side, depending on thickness.
2. Combine chopped onion, garlic, capers, olives and sun-dried tomatoes and chop them together. Put into a bowl and stir in vinegar and oil.
3. Add parsley, salt and pepper to salad and serve with fish, accompanied by lemon wedges.

Makes 4 servings.

Each serving contains:

Cal	Prot	Carb	Fib	Tot. Fat	Sat. Fat	Chol	Sodium
813	59g	6g	1g	61g	9g	162mg	543mg

GRILLED SALMON

Add sliced black olives to the tomato-parsley mixture, if desired.

*3 tablespoons virgin olive oil,
 plus extra for brushing*
3/4 cup (20g) basil leaves
Salt and pepper to taste

*2 salmon steaks, each about
 6 oz. (170g)*
2 large tomatoes, chopped
1 tablespoon chopped parsley

1. Preheat grill or broiler. Mix oil and basil in a blender until smooth. Add salt and pepper to taste; set aside.
2. Season salmon with salt and pepper and brush with oil. Grill or broil about 4 minutes on each side.
3. Combine tomatoes, parsley and salt and pepper to taste. Divide between 2 plates.
4. Top with salmon steaks and trickle with basil-oil mixture.

Makes 2 servings.

Each serving contains:

Cal	Prot	Carb	Fib	Tot. Fat	Sat. Fat	Chol	Sodium
578	35g	8g	2g	45g	6g	94mg	224mg

SICILIAN TUNA

Tuna fisheries have existed in southern Italy for centuries and were of major commercial importance, but now they are declining along with the size of the catch. Sicily is one place where there are still a number of fisheries, and this is a favorite Sicilian way of cooking tuna.

4 tablespoons olive oil
2 large onions, thinly sliced
4 tuna steaks, each 6-7 oz. (170-
*   200g) and 3/4 in. (2cm) thick*
1 tablespoon brown sugar

3 tablespoons red-wine vinegar
6 tablespoons (90ml) dry
*   white wine*
Salt and pepper to taste
Chopped parsley

1. Heat 3 tablespoons oil in a large skillet, add onions and sauté until soft. Increase heat and cook until onions are golden-brown. Using a slotted spoon, remove onions and set aside.
2. Add remaining oil to skillet. When it is hot, add tuna and fry briskly until browned on both sides. Lower heat for 1 minute before stirring in sugar, vinegar and wine.
3. Return onions to skillet to surround tuna. Season with salt and pepper, cover and cook over high heat 2 minutes.
4. Serve sprinkled with parsley.

Makes 4 servings.

Each serving contains:

Cal	Prot	Carb	Fib	Tot. Fat	Sat. Fat	Chol	Sodium
415	40g	10g	1g	22g	4g	77mg	249mg

SWORDFISH WITH SALMORIGLIO

Salmoriglio is a mixture of olive oil and herbs, and throughout Sicily it is brushed on fish steaks or pieces of fish threaded on skewers before they are grilled (preferably over a barbecue). The remaining dressing is served separately with the fish. Sicilians believe the only way to make salmoriglio is to add sea water; I make the nearest replica I can by using sea salt. Tuna can be used instead of swordfish.

1 small clove garlic
Sea salt
2 teaspoons minced parsley
1/4 teaspoon dried oregano
3/4 teaspoon minced rosemary

Juice of 1 small lemon
1/2 cup (125ml) virgin olive oil
Pepper to taste
4 swordfish steaks, each about
*   6 oz. (170g)*

1. Crush garlic with a pinch of sea salt. Using a fork, whisk in herbs and lemon juice. Still whisking, slowly pour in oil, then 2 tablespoons hot water, to make a thick sauce. Season with pepper.
2. Leave fish steaks whole or cut them into cubes and thread cubes onto skewers. Lay steaks or skewers in a shallow, nonmetallic dish. Pour sauce over, turn steaks or skewers over, then leave for 30 to 45 minutes, turning occasionally. (Whole steaks can be left for up to 1 hour.)
3. Preheat grill to fairly hot.
4. Grill skewers 6 to 7 minutes, turning occasionally, steaks about 4 minutes on each side, until flesh flakes when tested with a fork; brush with dressing when turning. Serve with remaining dressing.

Makes 4 servings.

Each serving contains:

Cal	Prot	Carb	Fib	Tot. Fat	Sat. Fat	Chol	Sodium
446	34g	0g	0g	34g	6g	66mg	220mg

SARDINES IN GRAPE LEAVES

The aroma of sardines cooking over a barbecue is one of the most evocative there is, especially when enhanced by the salty tang of sea air. If you do not have grape leaves, brush the fish with the garlic-parsley mixture before and during cooking.

12 fresh or preserved grape leaves
12 fresh sardines or herring
Salt and pepper to taste
2 cloves garlic, minced

1 cup parsley leaves, minced
Finely grated zest and juice
of 1 lemon

1. Preheat grill. If using preserved grape leaves, rinse them well under running hot water. Season sardines or herring with salt and pepper and wrap each one in a grape leaf.
2. Grill 3 to 4 minutes on each side.
3. Combine garlic, parsley, lemon zest, lemon juice, salt and pepper. Mix well.
4. Serve garlic-parsley mixture separately, to be eaten with each mouthful of fish.

Makes 4 servings.

Each serving contains:

Cal	Prot	Carb	Fib	Tot. Fat	Sat. Fat	Chol	Sodium
115	13g	3g	0g	6g	1g	38mg	129mg

SARDINES WITH LEMON AND OREGANO

Oregano is the herb that speaks most strongly of southern Italian cooking. Low bushes decked with white or pale-pink flowers can be seen growing wild on the hillsides throughout the summer. Bunches of oregano, flowers and all, are hung to dry in the warm sunshine because this is the one herb whose flavor develops when it is dried. Oregano is slightly minty and goes particularly well with oily fish such as sardines.

*3/4-1 lb. (340-450g) fresh
   sardines or herring
2-3 tablespoons virgin olive oil
1-1/2 tablespoons lemon juice*

*1-1/2 teaspoons dried oregano
Salt and pepper to taste
Lemon wedges*

1. Lay sardines or herring in a shallow, nonmetallic dish. Pour olive oil and lemon juice over them, sprinkle with half the oregano and season with salt and pepper. Turn fish, sprinkle with remaining oregano and season again. Let stand 10 to 30 minutes.
2. Preheat grill or broiler.
3. Grill or broil sardines 5 to 10 minutes, depending on size, turning them once or twice and brushing with marinade as they are turned. Serve with lemon wedges.

Makes 2 servings.

Each serving contains:

Cal	Prot	Carb	Fib	Tot. Fat	Sat. Fat	Chol	Sodium
537	41g	0g	0g	41g	7g	136mg	337mg

MULLET WITH PARMA HAM

If preferred, two whole fish can be used instead of fillets; put the sage or basil in the cavities of the fish and cook about 5 minutes on each side, depending on size.

4 mullet or mackerel fillets, each
   weighing 3-4 oz. (85-115g)
Freshly ground black pepper
4 sage leaves or large basil leaves

4 large slices of Parma ham
Olive oil
Fresh lemon juice

1. Season each fillet with pepper, place a sage or basil leaf on top, then wrap in a slice of Parma ham.
2. Heat a thin layer of oil in a large skillet. Add fish and cook gently about 3 minutes until ham is crisp. Turn fish and fry on the other side for 2 minutes.
3. Transfer fish to warm plates and squeeze lemon juice over them.

Makes 4 servings.

Each serving contains:

Cal	Prot	Carb	Fib	Tot. Fat	Sat. Fat	Chol	Sodium
303	34g	1g	0g	18g	4g	85mg	444mg

GRILLED SQUID WITH SPICY RELISH

Always use small squid for dishes such as this seacoast favorite!
Squid is often known by its Italian name, *calamari*.

6 fresh red chile peppers, seeded
4 cloves garlic
Leaves and fine stems from
  1/2 bunch of parsley
8-10 small squid (1 lb. / 450g)

2-3 tablespoons extra-virgin
  olive oil
Salt and pepper to taste
Lemon wedges

1. Mince chile peppers, setting aside 1 tablespoonful. Mince remaining peppers with garlic and parsley.
2. Slit squid bodies lengthwise in half and score undersides. Toss with reserved chile pepper, oil, salt and pepper. Let stand for 30 to 45 minutes.
3. Preheat grill or broiler to very hot. Grill or broil squid, scored side down first, about 2 minutes on each side until tender.
4. Serve with parsley-chile relish and lemon wedges.

Makes 4 servings.

Each serving contains:

Cal	Prot	Carb	Fib	Tot. Fat	Sat. Fat	Chol	Sodium
277	23g	12g	1g	16g	3g	318mg	492mg

BROILED SCALLOPS

If you do not have skewers, the scallops can be put on the broiler rack, but they will be more bother to turn over. Chunks of fresh firm fish such as cod, halibut or monkfish can also be prepared this way.

1 lb. (450g) scallops
Bay leaves
3 tablespoons extra-virgin
   olive oil
1-1/2 tablespoons lemon juice

2 teaspoons mixed chopped herbs,
   such as oregano, basil, parsley,
   fennel and chives
Salt and pepper to taste

1. Thread scallops onto skewers, alternating with bay leaves. Lay skewers in a shallow dish.
2. Combine oil, lemon juice, herbs, salt and pepper. Pour over scallops, turning to coat, and set aside for 30 minutes or at least while the broiler is heating.
3. Preheat broiler.
4. Broil scallops 4 to 5 minutes, turning occasionally and brushing with marinade as the skewers are turned.
5. Discard bay leaves and serve.

Makes 2 servings.

Each serving contains:

Cal	Prot	Carb	Fib	Tot. Fat	Sat. Fat	Chol	Sodium
300	18g	3g	0g	24g	3g	36mg	598mg

ABRUZZESE SHRIMP

Chile peppers are used in southern Italian cooking. They are the local spice of Abruzzo, where they are called *diavolicchio* ("little devil"). A dish described as *all'abruzzese* ("in the style of Abruzzo") will be generously flavored with them. The amount of chile in this dish is more restrained.

3 tablespoons virgin olive oil
1 red onion, minced
1 clove garlic, chopped
1/2 small dried red chile pepper, crumbled
2 tablespoons chopped parsley

1 lb. (450g) tomatoes, or
12 oz. (340g) canned tomatoes, chopped
1-1/4 lb. (575g) large shrimp in their shells
Salt to taste

1. Heat oil and cook onion until soft but not colored.
2. Add garlic and chile. Cook until garlic is lightly colored.
3. Stir in parsley, then add tomatoes and bring to a boil. Simmer steadily, uncovered, 15 to 20 minutes, stirring occasionally.
4. While sauce is cooking, peel shrimp. Add them to sauce, turn them over and cook about 4 minutes, stirring occasionally.
5. Season with salt and serve.

Makes 4 servings.

Each serving contains:

Cal	Prot	Carb	Fib	Tot. Fat	Sat. Fat	Chol	Sodium
213	19g	8g	2g	11g	2g	168mg	271mg

SHRIMP WITH CHILE AND GARLIC

This is a dish to serve to family or good friends, or people you know who will not mind abandoning knives and forks in favor of fingers. The best way to eat the shrimp is with your fingers—delicious but messy. Mop up the richly flavored juices with firm bread.

2 tablespoons olive oil
1/4 cup (60g) unsalted butter, diced
3 cloves garlic, crushed
1 dried red chile pepper, seeded and chopped

12 uncooked large shrimp in their shells
1 large lemon, quartered
Salt to taste

1. Heat oil and butter in a large, heavy skillet, add garlic, chile and shrimp and fry over high heat, shaking and tossing the pan constantly.
2. Add juice from half of lemon and salt. Serve immediately with the remaining lemon quarters.

Makes 2 servings.

Each serving contains:

Cal	Prot	Carb	Fib	Tot. Fat	Sat. Fat	Chol	Sodium
374	9g	4g	0g	37g	16g	132mg	219mg

BUTTERFLIED SHRIMP

The shrimp take only 3 minutes to cook but they do benefit from marinating for up to 30 minutes. So put them in the marinade before you start the rest of the meal, even if that only involves making a salad, setting the table and relaxing with a drink.

1 lb. (450g) jumbo shrimp in their shells
1/2 clove garlic, crushed
5 tablespoons virgin olive oil
4 tablespoons lemon juice

2 tablespoons sun-dried-tomato paste
1 tablespoon chopped basil
Small dash of chili sauce
Salt and pepper to taste

1. Remove heads and legs from shrimp. Using sharp scissors, cut shrimp almost in half lengthwise, leaving the tails intact. Put in a shallow dish and add garlic, 2 tablespoons oil and 2 tablespoons lemon juice. Stir together. Set aside for up to 30 minutes.
2. Preheat broiler or grill. Combine remaining oil and lemon juice, tomato paste, basil, chili sauce, salt and pepper.
3. Broil or grill shrimp about 3 minutes until they turn bright pink and have "butterflied." Serve them with tomato-chili sauce spooned over, or serve sauce in a small bowl for dipping.

Makes 2 to 4 servings.

Each serving contains:

Cal	Prot	Carb	Fib	Tot. Fat	Sat. Fat	Chol	Sodium
444	29g	2g	0g	35g	5g	269mg	513mg

Chapter Five

POULTRY AND MEAT

Italian chicken dishes have always found favor because they are invariably straightforward, simple and delicious. Chicken is also an obvious choice for the cook in a hurry as it is both quick cooking and versatile.

Although Italy has never been a great meat-eating nation, broiling and frying, the two cooking methods most frequently used for meat, combined with typically Italian simple, bold flavors are custom-made for meals that have to be prepared in a hurry. Use lean boneless cuts for tender, quickly cooked meat.

Try to have meat and poultry at room temperature before you start to cook them; not only will they cook more quickly, they will also be more succulent. The timings in my recipes are for room-temperature meat and poultry, so if you use colder products you will have to increase the cooking time.

PIQUANT CHICKEN AND CAPERS

The fresh, zingy flavors of capers and lemon turn plain chicken breasts into a light, piquant dish.

1 tablespoon olive oil

2 tablespoons (30g) unsalted butter

4 boneless chicken breasts, each about 5 oz. (145g)

Salt and pepper to taste

Finely grated zest and juice of 1 lemon

1 tablespoon capers, drained

1. Heat oil and butter in skillet. Flatten chicken breasts slightly with a meat mallet or the side of a large, heavy knife. Place in skillet, skin side down first, and sauté gently about 15 minutes until cooked and golden. Transfer to a warm plate, season with salt and pepper and keep warm.
2. Stir lemon zest and lemon juice into skillet, loosening and incorporating browned bits. Add capers and bring to a boil. Season and pour over the chicken.

Makes 4 servings.

Each serving contains:

				Tot.	Sat.		
Cal	Prot	Carb	Fib	Fat	Fat	Chol	Sodium
282	30g	0g	0g	17g	6g	101mg	219mg

ROSEMARY-LEMON CHICKEN

After an initial browning with rosemary and garlic, the chicken is cooked more gently with lemon juice and lemon zest so their flavor subtly impregnates its flesh.

1 tablespoon olive oil
2 tablespoons (30g) unsalted
 butter
1 sprig rosemary
1 clove garlic

4 boneless chicken breasts, each
 about 5 oz. (145g)
Juice and finely grated zest of
 1 lemon
Salt and pepper to taste

1. Heat oil, butter, rosemary and garlic in a skillet and cook gently 2 to 3 minutes.
2. Flatten chicken breasts slightly with a meat mallet or the side of a large, heavy knife. Increase heat under skillet, add chicken, skin side down first, and sauté 3 minutes on each side.
3. Pour lemon juice over chicken, add lemon zest, salt and pepper and cook over medium heat, turning chicken frequently, about 10 minutes. Discard rosemary and garlic.
4. Serve chicken with juices poured over.

Makes 4 servings.

Each serving contains:

Cal	Prot	Carb	Fib	Tot. Fat	Sat. Fat	Chol	Sodium
283	31g	0g	0g	17g	6g	101mg	140mg

BASIL CHICKEN

This is a beautiful dish to make in summer, when fresh basil is most fragrant. It is then well worth buying good-quality, fresh, traditionally reared free-range chicken.

4 skinless, boneless chicken
* breasts, each about*
* 5 oz. (145g)*
2 tablespoons (30g) unsalted
* butter*

1 tablespoon olive oil
Juice from 1 large lemon
1-1/2 handfuls basil leaves, torn
Salt and pepper to taste

1. Using a sharp knife, cut chicken breasts in half horizontally. Flatten them slightly with a meat mallet or the side of a large, heavy knife.
2. Heat butter and oil in a skillet that will hold the chicken in a single layer. Add chicken and sauté 3 to 4 minutes on each side.
3. Pour lemon juice over chicken, then add basil, salt and pepper. Turn chicken over and cook gently 2 to 3 minutes.
4. Serve chicken with sauce spooned over.

Makes 4 servings.

Each serving contains:

Cal	Prot	Carb	Fib	Tot. Fat	Sat. Fat	Chol	Sodium
233	29g	0g	0g	12g	5g	94mg	136mg

TUSCAN CHICKEN

This cooks gently for about 20 minutes so you have time to eat a first course or prepare a vegetable dish or a dessert. If desired, substitute white wine for some of the stock. Add more stock if it evaporates too quickly, or turn up the heat if there is some left.

1/4 cup (60g) butter
1/2 onion, minced
4 boneless chicken breasts, each
  5-6 oz. (145-170g)
1 cup (250ml) chicken stock

1/4 cup (60ml) fresh lemon juice
Salt and pepper to taste
2 egg yolks
Chopped fresh herbs, such as
  marjoram, basil, or thyme

1. Melt butter in a skillet that will hold the chicken in a single layer. Add onion and cook until softened.
2. Add chicken, skin side down, and brown lightly on both sides.
3. Pour stock over chicken and heat to simmering. Lower heat and simmer gently about 20 minutes, turning chicken occasionally until it is tender and there is no stock left.
4. Combine lemon juice, salt, pepper and egg yolks.
5. Remove pan from heat and immediately pour in lemon mixture, turning chicken quickly so it is coated with sauce; the heat of the chicken should set the egg. If desired, cover pan so egg heats a little longer. Garnish with chopped herbs and serve.

Makes 4 servings.

Each serving contains:

Cal	Prot	Carb	Fib	Tot. Fat	Sat. Fat	Chol	Sodium
388	39g	2g	0g	24g	11g	240mg	469mg

CHICKEN WITH SAVORY BASIL SAUCE

Basil leaves inserted underneath the skin of the chicken breasts add flavor during cooking. This flavoring is enhanced by the savory sauce, which is quickly and easily made while the chicken is cooking. The basil leaves can be inserted under the chicken skin ahead of time and the sauce can be made in advance.

Leaves from a 2-oz. (60g) bunch of basil
4 boneless chicken breasts with skin, each about 5 oz. (145g)
Salt and pepper to taste

1 clove garlic
4 teaspoons English mustard
4 tablespoons red-wine vinegar
6 anchovy fillets
3/4 cup (185ml) virgin olive oil

1. Preheat grill. Push 3 basil leaves under the skin of each chicken breast. Season breasts with salt and pepper. Grill, skin side up first, 6 to 8 minutes on each side.
2. With motor running, drop garlic clove into blender, then add mustard, vinegar, anchovy fillets and remaining basil. When just mixed, slowly pour in oil. Season with plenty of pepper.
3. Serve chicken with sauce.

Makes 4 servings.

Each serving contains:

Cal	Prot	Carb	Fib	Tot. Fat	Sat. Fat	Chol	Sodium
584	33g	3g	0g	49g	8g	91mg	486mg

CHICKEN-GORGONZOLA PARCELS

This popular recipe can easily be doubled for entertaining. It has a sophisticated Italian air, it is richly flavored but not heavily rich, and the preparation can be done ahead of time.

1-1/2 tablespoons (20g) unsalted
   butter, diced
1/2 clove garlic, minced
1 small shallot, minced
2 skinless, boneless chicken
   breasts, each about 5 oz. (145g)
1 teaspoon black-olive paste

2-oz. (60g) piece Gorgonzola
   cheese, cut in half
4 sage or basil leaves
Freshly ground black pepper
2 slices Parma ham
6 tablespoons (90ml) dry
   white wine

1. Heat butter in medium-size skillet, add garlic and shallot and cook gently until beginning to soften.
2. Cut a deep lengthwise pocket through the thick side of each chicken breast. Spread black-olive paste sparingly in each pocket and insert a piece of cheese. Place 2 sage or basil leaves on each breast, season with pepper, then wrap in a slice of Parma ham. Secure with wooden cocktail sticks or tie with string.
3. Using a slotted spoon, remove shallot mixture from skillet and reserve.
4. Add chicken to pan and cook about 2 minutes on each side.
5. Return shallot mixture to skillet, pour in wine and bring to boiling point. Cover tightly and cook gently about 12 minutes, until chicken is cooked through. Season with pepper.
6. Serve with cooking juices spooned over.

Makes 2 servings.

Each serving contains:

Cal	Prot	Carb	Fib	Tot. Fat	Sat. Fat	Chol	Sodium
416	41g	2g	0g	23g	12g	140mg	948mg

CHICKEN BREASTS IN SPINACH AND HAM

If you don't have enough chicken stock, make up the shortfall with water or wine. Save the stock that is left after cooking the chicken—it is well flavored and makes a good base for soups and casseroles.

2 large spinach leaves	*3 tablespoons virgin olive oil*
2 skinless, boneless chicken	*1 tablespoon walnut oil*
breasts, each about	*1 tablespoon tarragon vinegar*
5 oz. (145g)	*1-1/2 teaspoons chopped parsley*
Freshly ground black pepper	*1-1/2 tablespoons chopped dill*
2 slices Parma ham	*1/2 teaspoon dry English mustard*
1-1/2 cups (375ml) chicken stock	*Salt to taste*

1. Bring a saucepan of water to a boil. Remove stalks from spinach and discard. Add leaves to boiling water, cover and quickly return to boil. Remove from heat and drain.
2. Season each chicken breast with black pepper and wrap in a slice of Parma ham, then in a spinach leaf.
3. Bring stock to a boil in a saucepan that will hold the chicken breasts side by side. Add chicken breasts to pan; the loose end of each spinach leaf must be underneath. Cover and quickly return to boil. Turn down heat and poach 18 to 20 minutes.
4. Purée remaining ingredients in blender.
5. Serve the chicken on the sauce or pour the sauce over the chicken.

Makes 2 servings.

Each serving contains:

Cal	Prot	Carb	Fib	Tot. Fat	Sat. Fat	Chol	Sodium
470	39g	2g	1g	33g	5g	92mg	1163mg

CHICKEN WITH ZUCCHINI SAUCE

The flavor of virgin olive oil is an integral part of the sauce, but use a mild oil or the subtle flavor of the zucchini will be lost.

*4 boneless chicken breasts with
    skin, each about 6 oz. (170g)*
Salt and pepper to taste
2 tablespoons olive oil
1 small onion, minced

3/4 lb. (340g) small zucchini
2-3 tablespoons virgin olive oil
3 tablespoons chopped basil
2 teaspoons capers, chopped

1. Preheat broiler. Season chicken breasts with salt and pepper. Broil, skin side up first, 6 to 8 minutes on each side.
2. Heat olive oil in skillet and cook onion until beginning to soften.
3. While onion is cooking, coarsely grate zucchini. Add zucchini and 2 tablespoons water to onion. Cover and cook over low heat, stirring frequently, 8 to 10 minutes until zucchini is tender.
4. Place in food processor, add olive oil and process to a chunky purée. Return to skillet, add basil, capers, salt and pepper and heat through.
5. Serve chicken with sauce.

Makes 4 servings.

Each serving contains:

Cal	Prot	Carb	Fib	Tot. Fat	Sat. Fat	Chol	Sodium
409	38g	4g	1g	27g	5g	103mg	209mg

WARM CHICKEN-ZUCCHINI SALAD

Black olives, capers and sun-dried tomatoes combine with chicken breasts and steamed zucchini to make a satisfying, lively yet light, salad for lunch or supper.

8 pitted black olives, preferably
oil-cured
1 tablespoon capers
2 sun-dried tomato halves
1 small clove garlic
1-1/2 tablespoons white-wine
vinegar
Freshly ground black pepper

7 tablespoons (100ml) virgin
olive oil, plus extra for cooking
3 boneless chicken breasts with
skin, each about 5 oz. (145g)
1/2 lb. (225g) small zucchini,
sliced lengthwise
Crisp lettuce leaves
Small piece of Parmesan cheese

1. Chop olives with capers, sun-dried tomatoes and garlic. Mix with vinegar and pepper, then whisk in oil. Set aside.
2. Place each chicken breast in turn between 2 sheets of plastic wrap and beat with a rolling pin to flatten thoroughly.
3. Heat a heavy nonstick skillet and brush with oil. Add chicken breasts, skin side down first, and sauté 3 to 4 minutes on each side until brown and cooked through.
4. Bring a saucepan of water to a boil. Lay zucchini in a single layer, if possible, in a steaming basket, cover and steam 4 to 5 minutes until tender.
5. Divide lettuce leaves among 4 plates.
6. Cut chicken breasts into wide strips and toss with zucchini and dressing. Arrange on lettuce leaves. Using a potato peeler, shave thin slices of Parmesan over salad. Serve warm.

Makes 4 servings.

Each serving contains:

Cal	Prot	Carb	Fib	Tot. Fat	Sat. Fat	Chol	Sodium
401	25g	4g	1g	32g	6g	67mg	321mg

WARM CHICKEN SALAD

Skin on the chicken breasts helps to prevent the meat from drying out; if you do not want to eat the skin, discard it after cooking. For quicker cooking, use boneless chicken breasts and brush them with oil before cooking.

3 tablespoons virgin olive oil
1 tablespoon walnut oil
1 tablespoon balsamic vinegar
Salt and pepper to taste
Salad greens such as arugula,
  corn salad, frisee and Little
  Gem lettuce
4 small chicken breasts,
  preferably with skin

6 oz. (170g) broccoli florets
Olive oil
6 oz. (170g) oyster, shiitake or
  other large mushrooms, sliced
1/2 red bell pepper, chopped
1 bunch of chives, chopped

1. Preheat broiler and bring a saucepan of water to a boil. Combine oils, vinegar, salt and pepper. Put salad greens in a large salad bowl.
2. Broil chicken breasts, skin side up first, about 15 minutes, turning halfway through, until juices run clear when thickest part of breast is pierced with sharp knife.
3. Add broccoli to boiling water and cook until just tender. Drain.
4. Heat olive oil in skillet and sauté mushrooms and red pepper, stirring frequently so they remain crisp.
5. Slice chicken diagonally into strips. Remove mushrooms and pepper from skillet and toss with broccoli, chicken, greens and chives.
6. Stir dressing into skillet and bring to a boil. Pour over salad, toss lightly and serve.

Makes 4 servings.

Each serving contains:

Cal	Prot	Carb	Fib	Tot. Fat	Sat. Fat	Chol	Sodium
468	33g	5g	2g	35g	6g	86mg	154mg

PORK WITH SAGE

If you have time, marinate the pork in the lemon juice for 30 minutes. Chicken or turkey fillets can be substituted for the pork.

1 tablespoon olive oil
4 tablespoons (60g) unsalted
  butter
4 boneless pork steaks,
  each 4-5 oz. (115-145g)

Salt and pepper to taste
12 sage leaves, shredded
4 tablespoons fresh lemon juice

1. Heat oil and about 3 tablespoons butter in a skillet. Season pork with black pepper. Add pork and sage to skillet. Sauté until meat is browned on both sides and cooked through.
2. Transfer pork to a warm plate, season with salt and pepper and keep warm.
3. Pour most of fat from pan, leaving behind the sediment. Stir lemon juice into pan, loosening and incorporating browned bits, and bring to a boil. Lower heat and stir in remaining butter.
4. Return pork to skillet and turn once or twice in sauce before serving.

Makes 4 servings.

Each serving contains:

Cal	Prot	Carb	Fib	Tot. Fat	Sat. Fat	Chol	Sodium
349	32g	0g	0g	24g	11g	123mg	135mg

PORK WITH RED PEPPER AND GARLIC

I sometimes broil the red pepper as described on page 64. I add the pepper toward the end of cooking as it only needs a few minutes to heat through. If you have red peppers preserved in vinegar, you can use about 7 oz. (200g) drained peppers instead of the fresh one. They just have to be heated through, and the wine can be omitted.

3 tablespoons olive oil
3/4 lb. (340g) boneless pork,
   cut into chunks
2-3 cloves garlic, sliced
1 red bell pepper, thinly sliced

4 tablespoons dry white wine
Pinch of chile-pepper flakes or
   1/2 dried red chile pepper,
   crumbled, or chopped parsley
Salt and pepper to taste

1. Heat oil in a large skillet over high heat, then add the pork and cook, turning frequently, until browned.
2. Add garlic and red pepper, lower heat and cook 10 minutes or so, until pepper and pork are cooked. Add wine toward end of cooking; most of it should evaporate by the time the dish is ready.
3. Add chile-pepper flakes, chile or parsley, salt and pepper. Heat together briefly, then serve.

Makes 2 servings.

Each serving contains:

| | | | | Tot. | Sat. | | |
Cal	Prot	Carb	Fib	Fat	Fat	Chol	Sodium
481	39g	5g	1g	31g	7g	110mg	217mg

PORK OR VEAL WITH WHITE WINE

Traditionally, veal is cooked this way to add more "oomph" to the rather bland meat. Pork chops also benefit from the wine-and-sage treatment.

3 tablespoons olive oil
4 pork or veal steaks, each about
  5 oz. (145g)
10 sage leaves

2/3 cup (160ml) dry white wine
Salt and freshly ground black
  pepper

1. Heat oil in a large, heavy skillet, then add pork or veal and cook until brown on both sides. Add sage leaves toward the end.
2. Stir wine into pan and bring to a boil. Lower heat and cook 10 to 15 minutes, turning meat over halfway through.
3. Transfer meat to warm plates. If necessary, boil remaining wine to thicken sauce. Season, pour over meat and serve.

Makes 4 servings.

Each serving contains:

Cal	Prot	Carb	Fib	Tot. Fat	Sat. Fat	Chol	Sodium
333	32g	0g	0g	19g	5g	92mg	135mg

VEAL SCALLOPS WITH BASIL

This is an adaptation of veal Milanese. To give the classic dish more flavor, I add Parmesan cheese to the breadcrumbs and basil to the egg, and I squeeze lemon juice over the veal before cooking. Sometimes I also deglaze the pan with lemon juice. Mashed potatoes and fennel or zucchini are good accompaniments.

Fresh lemon juice
4 veal scallops, each about
  2 oz. (60g)
3 basil leaves, finely shredded
Salt to taste
1 egg

2 tablespoons freshly grated
  Parmesan cheese
Pepper to taste
4 tablespoons dry breadcrumbs
Olive oil and butter for frying
Lemon wedges

1. Squeeze lemon juice over veal. Using a fork, beat basil and salt into egg. Mix Parmesan cheese and pepper into breadcrumbs.
2. Dip each veal scallop into egg, to coat lightly on both sides, then in breadcrumbs. Pat breadcrumbs lightly in place, then shake off excess.
3. Heat a little oil and butter in a large, heavy skillet over moderately high heat. Add veal in a single layer and cook until brown on one side. Turn and cook until just golden.
4. Drain on paper towels. Serve with lemon wedges.

Makes 2 servings.

Each serving contains:

Cal	Prot	Carb	Fib	Tot. Fat	Sat. Fat	Chol	Sodium
361	28g	10g	1g	23g	9g	210mg	516mg

LAMB CUTLETS WITH ROSEMARY

Allow as much time as possible for step 1, so the lamb can absorb the flavors of the garlic, oil and lemon juice, in typical Italian fashion.

1 clove garlic
Salt and pepper to taste
3 tablespoons virgin olive oil, plus
*   extra for brushing*

1 tablespoon lemon juice
2 lamb chops, 1 inch (2.5cm)
*   thick*
A few sprigs of rosemary

1. Finely crush garlic with a pinch of salt, then mix with oil, lemon juice and pepper. Brush over lamb; set aside 30 to 60 minutes, if possible, or at least while broiler is heating.
2. Preheat broiler. Lay rosemary sprigs on broiler rack and put chops on top. Broil 1 minute on each side, brushing chops with oil as they are turned. Reduce heat slightly and cook lamb for 4 minutes without turning.
3. Season with salt and serve.

Makes 2 servings.

Each serving contains:

Cal	Prot	Carb	Fib	Tot. Fat	Sat. Fat	Chol	Sodium
472	40g	0g	0g	33g	7g	128mg	246mg

LAMB WITH PEPERONATA

In the traditional recipe for *peperonata*, the vegetables are cooked slowly until they are softened and their flavors combined. Here they are cooked quickly, so they retain their shape and the individual flavors remain distinct. You can replace some of the red or yellow peppers with green pepper, if desired. Peperonata also goes well with grilled beef and pork.

1 tablespoon olive oil, plus extra
for brushing
1 small onion, minced
1 clove garlic, chopped
1 red bell pepper
1 yellow bell pepper
1 tomato

Pinch of chopped rosemary
1/2 cup (125ml) vegetable stock
1 teaspoon sun-dried-tomato
paste
4 lamb steaks, each 6-8 oz.
(170-225g)
Salt and pepper to taste

1. Preheat grill or broiler. Heat oil in a skillet and cook onion and garlic until soft and transparent; do not allow them to color.
2. Seed and chop peppers and tomato.
3. Add peppers to skillet and cook about 1 minute. Stir in tomato and rosemary. After a few seconds add stock and tomato paste. Boil until peppers are tender-crisp.
4. While peperonata is cooking, season one side of each steak with pepper and brush with olive oil. Grill or broil about 4 minutes, depending on thickness, until brown and cooked as desired. Season the second side of each steak and brush with oil when turning the lamb over.
5. Season peperonata with salt and pepper and serve with the lamb.

Makes 4 servings.

Each serving contains:

Cal	Prot	Carb	Fib	Tot. Fat	Sat. Fat	Chol	Sodium
692	46g	8g	2g	52g	19g	179mg	217mg

LAMB CUTLETS WITH HERBS

You can make this for four people by doubling the ingredients, providing you can fit all the cutlets beneath the broiler. To add a light garlic flavor, rub the cutlets with a halved garlic clove before seasoning them with pepper.

1-1/2 tablespoons (20g) butter,
*   chopped*
1 tablespoon virgin olive oil
6 lamb cutlets, each about
*   4 oz. (115g)*

Pepper to taste
Handful of chopped fresh herbs,
*   such as mint, marjoram, basil,*
*   parsley, thyme and rosemary*
Salt to taste

1. Preheat broiler. Heat butter and oil in a small saucepan.
2. Season lamb cutlets with pepper and brush both sides with oil-butter mixture. Place on broiler rack and sprinkle tops of cutlets with half of herbs. Broil 2 to 3 minutes, depending on how well you like lamb to be cooked.
3. Turn cutlets over, brush with juices from broiler pan and sprinkle with remaining herbs. Broil 2 to 3 minutes.
4. Transfer to warm plates. Top with pan juices and salt to taste.

Makes 2 servings.

Each serving contains:

Cal	Prot	Carb	Fib	Tot. Fat	Sat. Fat	Chol	Sodium
985	68g	0g	0g	77g	33g	292mg	428mg

STEAK WITH TOMATOES AND OLIVES

Aim for 12 slices of steak; if you buy the meat from a butcher, he can slice it for you. If you slice the meat yourself, you will find it easier if it is really cold. Use a very sharp knife. You could use minute steaks; cook them 1 to 2 minutes on each side.

3 tablespoons olive oil, plus extra
    for brushing
1 small onion, minced
2 cloves garlic, choppped
2 tomatoes, seeded and chopped
Small handful of pitted black
    olives, halved or quartered

Pinch of dried oregano
Pepper to taste
1 lb. (450g) beef steak, thinly
    sliced
Salt to taste
Chopped parsley

1. Heat oil in a skillet, add onion and cook until softened and lightly colored. Add garlic toward the end of cooking.
2. Add tomatoes, olives, oregano and pepper and simmer about 15 minutes.
3. While sauce is cooking, heat another skillet, brush with oil, then quickly fry meat just long enough to brown it.
4. Season meat with salt and pepper and slip into sauce. Turn meat, baste a few times with sauce, and serve sprinkled with chopped parsley.

Makes 4 servings.

Each serving contains:

Cal	Prot	Carb	Fib	Tot. Fat	Sat. Fat	Chol	Sodium
358	27g	7g	1g	25g	5g	77mg	182mg

STEAK WITH GARLIC AND HERBS

This is an ideal treatment for good-quality steaks, although it does not qualify for the title *Fiorentenina*. This famous Tuscan dish is made from thick T-bone steaks from Tuscan-reared Val di Chiana cattle, which have a unique quality, flavor and texture.

4 sirloin steaks, each about
  6 oz. (170g)
2 cloves garlic, halved
Virgin olive oil
Pepper to taste

2 tablespoons chopped mixed
  herbs, such as parsley, thyme,
  marjoram and basil
Salt to taste
4 lemon wedges

1. Preheat broiler or grill. Rub steaks thoroughly with cut sides of garlic and brush with oil. Season with pepper.
2. Broil or grill steaks 2 to 4 minutes on each side until done as desired.
3. Sprinkle with herbs and salt and serve accompanied by lemon wedges.

Makes 4 servings.

Each serving contains:

Cal	Prot	Carb	Fib	Tot. Fat	Sat. Fat	Chol	Sodium
323	39g	0g	0g	17g	5g	115mg	152mg

STEAK PIZZAIOLA

Oregano is the traditional herb to use for this southern Italian dish. If it is not available replace it with 3 tablespoons chopped parsley. Depending on time and preference, peel the tomatoes.

3 tablespoons olive oil
4 thin sirloin or rump steaks,
   each 5-6 oz. (145-170g)
2 cloves garlic, crushed
1-1/4 lb. (575g) tomatoes,
   chopped

2 sprigs fresh oregano or
   4 teaspoon dried oregano
3 tablespoons chopped basil
Salt and pepper to taste

1. Heat oil in skillet, add steaks and fry over high heat about 2 minutes on each side.
2. Add garlic to skillet, fry until fragrant, then add tomatoes, oregano, basil, salt and pepper. Cook 3 to 5 minutes, until tomatoes have softened and juices have reduced slightly.

Makes 4 servings.

Each serving contains:

Cal	Prot	Carb	Fib	Tot. Fat	Sat. Fat	Chol	Sodium
383	41g	7g	1g	21g	5g	115mg	165mg

SAUSAGES WITH POLENTA

Polenta makes an enticingly savory, warming and rustic "porridge." It is a perfect accompaniment to hearty casseroles, or the basis of a range of tasty dishes. Quick-cooking polenta is worth keeping on hand for occasions when you want something quick to make and satisfying and interesting to eat.

2 tablespoons olive oil
1 lb. (450g) hot Italian sausages, cut into 3-inch (7.5cm) lengths
4 oz. (115g) sliced pancetta or thick-cut bacon, cut into strips
1 small onion, minced
8-10 oz. (225-280g) fresh mushrooms, chopped

1-1/2 large tomatoes, seeded and chopped
10 oz. (280g) quick-cooking polenta
Salt and pepper to taste
Shredded basil or chopped parsley
Freshly grated Parmesan cheese

1. Heat oil in large skillet; add sausages and pancetta or bacon. Add onion.
2. When sausages are brown and fat is beginning to run from pancetta or bacon, remove from skillet and set aside. Add mushrooms to pan and cook 2 to 3 minutes, then add tomatoes.
3. Return meats to pan and cook about 15 minutes.
4. Cook polenta according to package directions. Pour into a warm, large dish and make a well in the center.
5. Add salt and pepper to sauce in skillet and pour, with meat, onto polenta. Garnish with basil or parsley and cheese.

Makes 4 servings.

Each serving contains:

Cal	Prot	Carb	Fib	Tot. Fat	Sat. Fat	Chol	Sodium
605	25g	58g	4g	30g	9g	58mg	876mg

Chapter Six

DESSERTS

Fresh fruit has always been a favorite way of ending a meal in Italy—hardly surprising when you think of the luscious, flavor-packed produce Italians have on their doorsteps. Try ripe pears with some glowing, fresh fontina cheese, perhaps adding some walnuts in their shells for an autumn dessert. Pears also go well with Gorgonzola, while plump, juicy black grapes are a good partner for taleggio.

The fruit is often eaten plain, but it can easily be made into something more special. Mascarpone with Fruit, for example, is particularly satisfying following a light meal. Or try Summer Berries, the surprise ingredient of which is a dash of black pepper.

For a richer dessert, indulge in Marsala Raisin Fritters. Or simply finish your meal with a small glass of lusciously sweet vin santo into which you dip crisp, dry almonds.

GRAPES, WALNUTS AND FONTINA

The walnuts need to be as fresh as possible and the cheese the best quality you can find. Serve a generous quantity for people to help themselves.

8 oz. (225g) fontina cheese   *3/4 lb. (340g) walnuts in shells*
1 lb. (450g) white grapes   *Crusty Italian bread*

1. Put cheese in center of large serving plate.
2. Divide grapes into small bunches and arrange around cheese. Add walnuts.
3. Serve with crusty bread.

Makes 4 servings.

Each serving contains:

Cal	Prot	Carb	Fib	Tot. Fat	Sat. Fat	Chol	Sodium
547	21g	28g	2g	42g	13g	66mg	460mg

MERINGUE-TOPPED STUFFED PEACHES

Amaretti biscuits are Italian almond-flavored meringue cookies. Wrapped in twos, they are usually sold in colorful tins.

6 amaretti biscuits
Dash of nutmeg
4 fresh peaches, halved and
    peeled, or 8 well-drained
    canned peach halves

2 egg whites
2 tablespoons sugar
Sliced toasted almonds or
    chopped candied fruit

1. Preheat oven to 425F (220C). Leaving amaretti in their wrappers, crush with a rolling pin. Remove from wrappers, add a dash of nutmeg and toss to mix.
2. Place peaches, cut side up, in a baking dish. Fill peach halves with amaretti crumbs.
3. Whip egg whites until frothy; continue beating and slowly add sugar. Beat until stiff and glossy.
4. Spoon meringue over peaches. Top with almonds or candied fruit and bake 8 to 10 minutes or until golden. Serve at once.

Makes 4 servings.

Each serving contains:

Cal	Prot	Carb	Fib	Tot. Fat	Sat. Fat	Chol	Sodium
250	5g	42g	4g	8g	4g	0mg	122mg

MARSALA RAISIN FRITTERS

Try to use Marsala for this Sicilian recipe. It marries particularly well with raisins and gives the authentic taste to the fritters. Be sure to use sweet Marsala, not dry.

1/3 cup (50g) raisins
2/3 cup (160ml) sweet Marsala
* or sweet sherry*
2 cups (250g) all-purpose flour

2 egg yolks
2/3 cup (160ml) milk
Vegetable oil for frying
Sugar

1. Macerate raisins in Marsala or sherry 15 minutes.
2. Put flour in large bowl and make a well in center. Stir in egg yolks, raisins, soaking liquid and enough milk to make a batter with the consistency of heavy cream.
3. Heat a 1-inch (2.5cm) layer of oil in large skillet. Use about three tablespoons batter for each fritter. Fry 3 or 4 fritters at a time about 5 minutes until golden, turning once.
4. Remove with slotted spoon and drain on paper towels. Repeat until all batter is used.
5. Sprinkle hot fritters with sugar and serve immediately.

Makes 4 servings.

Each serving contains:

Cal	Prot	Carb	Fib	Tot. Fat	Sat. Fat	Chol	Sodium
519	10g	69g	2g	18g	3g	112mg	29mg

BERRIES IN RED WINE

Use any combination of fresh berries in this simple elegant dessert.

2 cups (450g) blackberries or
   raspberries
Sugar to taste (optional)

4 glasses Italian red wine
Cantucci or biscotti cookies

1. Divide berries among 4 individual serving dishes. If berries are not sweet, sprinkle with sugar to taste.
2. Pour wine over berries. Serve with cookies.

Makes 4 servings.

Each serving contains:

Cal	Prot	Carb	Fib	Tot. Fat	Sat. Fat	Chol	Sodium
122	1g	11g	3g	0g	0g	0mg	6mg

Cantucci ~ *These crisp, dry almond cookies can be found in specialty Italian food stores. Other light, crisp cookies can be used instead.*

Biscotti ~ *These very crisp Italian cookies are often used for dipping in dessert wine or coffee. They are baked twice, first in a loaf, then in slices, and flavorful additions may include anise seed, hazelnuts or almonds.*

SUMMER BERRIES

Enjoy sweet-and-spicy fresh berries prepared the Italian way.

1 tablespoon Galliano liqueur
1/4 cup (60ml) honey

2 cups (450g) fresh blackberries
or raspberries
Dash black pepper

1. Stir Galliano into honey until well combined.
2. Place berries in a deep bowl, pour honey mixture over berries, sprinkle with a dash of black pepper. Gently stir to coat.
3. Taste and add more pepper, if desired.

Makes 4 servings.

Each serving contains:

Cal	Prot	Carb	Fib	Tot. Fat	Sat. Fat	Chol	Sodium
115	1g	28g	3g	0g	0g	0mg	1mg

STRAWBERRIES WITH BALSAMIC VINEGAR

Although this has become quite a trendy dessert, sprinkling rich balsamic vinegar over fruit or berries to highlight their flavor has been done in Modena, the home of balsamic vinegar, for a long time.

1 lb. (450g) fresh strawberries,   3-4 tablespoons balsamic vinegar
  halved if large   Sugar to taste (optional)

1. Put strawberries in serving bowl or in 4 individual serving dishes.
2. Sprinkle with balsamic vinegar. Gently turn and stir strawberries. Let stand about 10 minutes.
3. Taste and sprinkle with sugar, if desired.

Makes 4 servings.

Each serving contains:

Cal	Prot	Carb	Fib	Tot. Fat	Sat. Fat	Chol	Sodium
39	1g	10g	2g	0g	0g	0mg	1mg

MASCARPONE WITH FRUIT

While fresh fruit is always preferred, well-drained canned fruit is quite acceptable for this quick dessert.

4 fresh apricots or plums, halved, pitted
4-6 tablespoons mascarpone or ricotta cheese

1 cup (225g) fresh raspberries or blueberries
Brown sugar

1. Divide apricot or plum halves among 4 individual serving plates.
2. Spoon cheese into fruit cavities. Top with berries and sprinkle with brown sugar.

Makes 4 servings.

Each serving contains:

Cal	Prot	Carb	Fib	Tot. Fat	Sat. Fat	Chol	Sodium
244	4g	12g	2g	20g	14g	53mg	10mg

Mascarpone cheese ~ *This triple-cream cheese is extremely rich and quite expensive. A favorite with Italians, it may be difficult to find in the U.S. and Canada. For an acceptable substitute, use 3 ounces cream cheese mixed with 5 tablespoons whipping cream or 3 ounces ricotta cheese mixed with 3 tablespoons whipping cream.*

ORANGE-POACHED PEARS

The delicate flavor of pears is enhanced by orange juice and wine.

2/3 cup (150g) sugar
1-1/2 cups (375ml) orange juice
1 tablespoon grated orange peel
1/2 cup (125ml) dry vermouth or
  white wine
1 cinnamon stick

4 firm, ripe pears, peeled, each
  cut into 8 slices
1/2 cup (125ml) whipping cream,
  whipped
Toasted chopped hazelnuts

1. In a deep saucepan heat sugar, orange juice, orange peel, vermouth or wine and cinnamon stick.
2. Add pears, cover and simmer 15 to 20 minutes, until tender. Remove cinnamon stick and discard.
3. Place pears in 4 dessert bowls. Top each with 3 tablespoons cooking liquid, a dollop of whipped cream and a sprinkle of hazelnuts.

Makes 6 to 8 servings.

Each serving contains:

Cal	Prot	Carb	Fib	Tot. Fat	Sat. Fat	Chol	Sodium
259	1g	48g	3g	5g	2g	14mg	6mg

ITALIAN RASPBERRY LAYER

If you can, make this dessert before you begin to prepare the rest of the meal, so the flavor has time to develop. It is also good made with blueberries.

3/4 cup (170g) ricotta cheese
6 tablespoons mascarpone or
cream cheese
2 tablespoons powdered sugar

Rose water
2 cups (450g) raspberries
Toasted hazelnuts

1. Sieve ricotta cheese or beat it in a bowl. Stir in mascarpone or cream cheese, sugar and rose water.
2. Reserve a few raspberries for decoration. Alternate spoonfuls of cheese mixture and berries in individual dishes. Chill for up to 30 minutes, then decorate with reserved berries and hazelnuts.

Makes 4 servings.

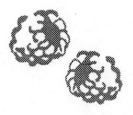

Each serving contains:

Cal	Prot	Carb	Fib	Tot. Fat	Sat. Fat	Chol	Sodium
340	9g	12g	3g	28g	18g	76mg	46mg

CAPPUCCINO CREAMS

Make this first, as the flavor improves if it has time to mellow.

2 tablespoons rum or brandy
1-2 tablespoons espresso-grind
  coffee

1/2-1 tablespoon powdered sugar
1 cup (225g) ricotta cheese
Grated bitter chocolate

1. Stir rum or brandy, coffee and sugar into cheese; beat well.
2. Place in 4 individual dishes or glasses and decorate generously with chocolate. Chill for up to 2 hours, if possible.

Makes 4 servings.

Each serving contains:

Cal	Prot	Carb	Fib	Tot. Fat	Sat. Fat	Chol	Sodium
178	7g	8g	0g	10g	6g	31mg	89mg

ICE CREAM WITH ESPRESSO

Scoop ice cream into balls and return to freezer to harden.

8 scoops vanilla or chocolate
  ice cream
4 cups (1 liter) warm espresso or
  strong coffee

Whipped cream (optional)
4 almond or chocolate biscotti

1. Place ice cream in 4 tall glasses. Pour in coffee.
2. Add a dollop of whipped cream, if desired.
3. Serve with biscotti.

Makes 4 servings.

Each serving contains:

Cal	Prot	Carb	Fib	Tot. Fat	Sat. Fat	Chol	Sodium
335	6g	46g	1g	16g	9g	66mg	150mg

INDEX